Latin Superfoods

100 Simple, Delicious, and Energizing Recipes for Total Health

Leticia Moreinos Schwartz

Skyhorse Publishing

Skyhorse Publishing books may be purchased in bulk at special discounts for sales promotion, corporate gifts, fund-raising, or educational purposes. Special editions can also be created to specifications. For details, contact the Special Sales Department, Skyhorse Publishing, 307 West 36th Street, 11th Floor, New York, NY 10018 or info@skyhorsepublishing.com.

Skyhorse® and Skyhorse Publishing® are registered trademarks of Skyhorse Publishing, Inc.®, a Delaware corporation.

Visit our website at www.skyhorsepublishing.com.

10 9 8 7 6 5 4 3 2 1

Library of Congress Cataloging-in-Publication Data is available on file.

Cover design by Laura Klynstra
Cover photos by Michelle Fonseca and Leticia Moreinos Schwartz

Print ISBN: 978-1-5107-4595-7
Ebook ISBN: 978-1-5107-4597-1

Printed in China

To my parents, who instilled in me the love for food and health; to my husband Dean, and my beautiful children who fill my life with love; and to all immigrants, from all over the world, who like me, came to this country with a dream of a better life for themselves and their children.

Contents

Introduction 1

My Cooking Philosophy 6

My Eating Philosophy 10

Guide to SuperFoods 13

Flavored Waters, Juices, Smoothies & Bowls 27

Appetizers 45

Salads and Soups 79

Poultry 111

Fish 149

Side Dishes and Bowls 171

Desserts 199

Acknowledgments 221

Conversion Charts 222

Index 223

Introduction

Welcome to my world—a world in which healthy cooking is oxygen!

Many people associate healthy cooking with boring taste and flavorless foods. I'm on a mission to prove that healthy eating can be not only absolutely delicious, but also that food is medicine, and that by living a healthy lifestyle you can take control of your health and of your life.

Having a personal connection with type 2 diabetes—my grandfather died from complications of the disease—I've learned to pay attention to nutrition, eating habits, and lifestyle. For the past five years, I've been on an incredible journey as the spokesperson for America's Diabetes Challenge, a campaign that raises awareness about diabetes and management techniques through healthy living. I see firsthand that unhealthy eating habits can contribute to serious health issues.

What I quickly realized while traveling around the country, is that immigrants—including myself—are especially vulnerable to dietary and lifestyle diseases. Once we move to the US, our habits change for the worse, along with our health. We no longer shop at farmer's markets or cook home-made meals. Instead, we buy take-out and pre-packed foods. The road from a healthy Latin culture to the North American table became a tough one somewhere along the way.

The Latin Revolution

The good news is that maintaining a healthy diet has never been easier, in part because of the influence of Latin culture in this country.

Let's start with juices and smoothies. Fruits and vegetable juices have always flowed in the veins of Latinos. Jamba Juice pioneered the trend in the US, and many clones have since invaded American cities. You will find tons of healthy juices in this book! See page 27 for more.

Tacos, tapas, quesadillas, and guacamole are no longer exclusive to Latin culture, but are familiar to most Americans. They are here too! Quinoa (typical to Peruvian cooking) is sold in just about any supermarket, along with plantains, yucca, and cilantro. Try my Quinoa Risotto with Peas and Turkey Bacon (page 181) and you'll be making it over and over again. What about kale, avocados, and açaí? All Latin. All healthy. All Superfoods—and all here in this book, with amazing recipes to showcase their super powers.

In Search of Flavors

I was born and raised in Brazil, a country that neighbors almost every other country in South America. Having had the chance to travel through South America and immerse myself in Latin culture, I've met chefs and home cooks from all walks of life. After graduating from the International Culinary Center in New York (formerly the French Culinary Institute), I was lucky to work with amazing chefs and learned an incredible amount from them.

At La Caravelle in New York, we cooked elaborate recipes from the French repertoire; today it's all about simplicity. Recently, I helped Chef Eric Di Domenico, La Caravelle's former chef, prepare a dinner party where he served a delicious tapioca pearl pudding that was light, healthy, and full of tropical flavors (you can try my version on page 212).

As a food writer, I've also had the chance to work with and interview chefs and home cooks in Latin America. Chef Daniel Biron from Teva, a restaurant in Rio small in space, but huge in cultural impact, urged me to taste his farofa. He prepares a mixture of garlic and Brazil nuts that transforms the whole taste of farofa (see page 185 for my healthy take on this dish).

My radar for treasured recipes is always on, and sometimes the most amazing Latin chefs are cooking recipes that don't necessarily have a Latin stamp on it. When I ate at Estella in New York City, my heart pounded for every bite of food, and I was overjoyed to discover that Ignacio Mattos is Uruguayan. That's the beauty of cooking: finding the light in every ingredient, even the most ordinary ones—like celery.

In fact, most of the recipes in this cookbook are prepared with ingredients just like celery: simple, ordinary, easy to find, but with amazing super powers! Precisely because they are so trivial, they are also overlooked and underexplored. In my way of cooking, it's just a matter of doing interesting things with them. The Orange Salad with Pumpkin Seeds and Crumbled *Queso-Blanco* on page 93 is an eye-opening recipe! Same with a Watermelon Carpaccio with Feta Cheese, Olives, Cilantro, and Arugula on page 107, and many more throughout the book!

This cookbook is my contribution to more healthful eating, with fully tested and re-tested recipes, some gluten-free, some vegan, and lots of lean proteins. I take traditional Latin dishes and find ways to make them even healthier.

The Home Cooking Revolution

Beyond offering a range of recipes to fit any palate, this book imparts a philosophy of joyful cooking. My mission is to inspire you to take full responsibility of your own well-being and to eat better and cook frequently, so that you can generate health, energy, and vigor for yourself and your family.

Healthy is for everyone! Whether you're just starting to cook, or refreshing your cooking repertoire, these recipes have everything you need to create a lifestyle you love.

Second Nature

My two teenagers are perpetually hungry; they want big dinners, big portions, and lots of flavors. Over time, I slowly switched recipes that originally called for red meat to leaner types of protein. Today, I make Picadillo with chicken (page 139) instead of beef. Same with Ropa Vieja—a classic Cuban dish which is a favorite with my kids—as the chicken shreds so beautifully (page 115). You will find tons of recipes featuring lean proteins in this book that make great weeknight meals.

And the best part is that my kids don't even think about the fact that the recipes they're eating are diabetes-friendly and super healthy. When I told them that the brownies are gluten-free, they raised their heads and said, "Really?" Then they went back to enjoying a delicious brownie, that just happened to be gluten-free. That's the spirit I instilled in our cooking life. You don't have to sacrifice flavor when preparing healthy recipes.

The process by which I selected the recipes for this book descends into a few main issues that are an integral part of my life: taste, health, convenience, culture, education, and lifestyle. As a true bi-continental chef, I want to provide life-changing, long-lasting accessible recipes. Yes, that is a great recipe, but can I really say that it will change your life? Yes, that's the goal! Small changes add up! Cook up! Wise up!

One reason writing a book is so challenging is that there is no real metric for greatness, or best taste, or deliciousness—the recipes in this book are really special to me, because they have all helped steer the health course of my own family.

As a family, we eat a lot of grains, nuts, seeds, fruits and vegetables, and lean proteins. It's second nature for us. In this book, I offer you recipes with plenty of the same, along with interesting ideas, deep flavors, and simple preparations which makes them perfect for a healthy lifestyle.

Where else would you find Broccoli Fajitas (page 192), or Spinach Mushroom Quesadillas (page 71) that even picky little eaters will love? All of these recipes have inspired me, along with friends, family, and hundreds of people who take my cooking

classes and have helped me reimagine and redefine a term of convention that we sometimes lose sight of: cooking is health.

This is what great cooking does—it seizes us, it comforts us, it forces us to see what's beneath the body we have, the blood that runs in our veins. The world needs chefs and cookbook authors who shake us from our torpor and remind us that what we cook, isn't all there is to be cooked.

In this book, what makes a great recipe is not merely the ability to present us with different foods to cook, but the ability to inspire us to create a different world of our choosing.

About the Recipes

The recipes in this book were tested and retested many times, but when it comes to cooking and eating, you need to make your own judgment. For example, while so many juices are incredibly delicious, when and how you drink them makes all the difference. I drink juices in the morning on an empty stomach and I wait at least an hour before I eat breakfast. That juice has a completely different impact than if I were drinking it as a side to a meal. Be conscious about eating habits. It's not only what you eat, but how much and, perhaps most importantly, at what time, that counts.

The same thing goes for cooking. While I may write, "cook the garlic until it's just golden, about two minutes," on your stove, it might only take one minute, or it might take five. Adapt these recipes to your kitchen, to your appliances, and to your life.

These recipes have helped shape the story of my family; I hope they will help you shape your story as well!

A Cookbook in Your Hands

Sometimes, it's not enough to love something. You have to take that thing—stories, recipes, cooking, photos—and do more than love it. It needs to have a home. While I can easily admit that I'm fascinated by the cooking industry, it is no secret to anyone who's in our business, or any business, that print publishing is infinitely more difficult today than it was a decade ago. And yet, we want it. We do it. Because of the satisfaction of making something, of taking my own photos, styling my own food, writing stories behind my recipes, and arguing over how much salt will taste better. The actual holding of this book in your hands, turning the pages, feeling its weight, still fulfills some elemental need that humans have to assemble something with our hands and our eyes. Call it old fashioned. But it's here. And we're cooking! Cheers to that!

Connections

If you want more inspiration as you dive into *Latin Superfoods*, the book and the mission, be sure to check out my blog chefleticia.com and my Instagram page @leticiamorein osschwartz for continued support, updates, and even more recipes. The blog started as a way to give home to a community of readers interested in food and culture. I'd love for you to be part of it as you begin your own journey to eat better and feel better!

My Cooking Philosophy

As the spokesperson for a campaign that focuses on healthy living and having had the opportunity to talk to thousands of people who struggle for a healthier lifestyle, one of the most common problems I hear is, "I work too much, come home late, and don't have time to cook." This phrase alone is probably one of the biggest reasons why I decided to write this book.

Cooking is a language, a way of communicating not just something about the way we eat, but the world we live in. Cooking is a democratic art. We all eat a few times a day, and it remains the single most effective way to connect body, heart, and soul with health. What we choose to eat is part of what we are, and also part of what we would like to be.

But eating and cooking aren't necessarily the same thing. The two are of course typically associated together, but they are two different acts, and I'll admit that I get a lot more satisfaction from the act of cooking

than from the act of eating. Cooking feeds my soul. Eating feeds my body.

But to cook, we need time. And nobody has time. We *make* time. Time is a gift, like cooking is a gift. These are some of the most valuable gifts you can give yourself: taking time to be responsible for your own well-being. When you cook, you have control of what goes into your body—therefore you have control of your health. What can be more important than that?

"Time is free, but it's priceless. You can't own it. But you can use it. You can't keep it, but you can spend it. Once it's lost, you never get it back." Words to live by, spoken by *New York Times* bestselling author Harvey MacKay.

When it comes to cooking, we need to change our perception of time. My goal in this book is to help you change your mind toward coming home from a full work day and having to prepare dinner.

Instead of looking at the kitchen as a burden, where you have to prep, cook, eat, and clean, I encourage you to look at time through self-improvement and use healthy cooking as a tool for that. I challenge you to enter the kitchen with a different perspective: turn on the music, put on an apron, and see cooking as a source of health, a way of relaxation, family gathering, therapy; a place where you can sing and dance, talk, and even exercise—while cooking an amazing healthy meal!

Here are some of the ways that we can make time for cooking.

Cook on the Weekends and Freeze Meals for the Week

Plan your meals for the week ahead of time and prepare them during the weekend. It really works. Just a few hours on a Sunday afternoon can change the way you eat and ultimately feel during the week. It also allows you to try new recipes and avoid the scramble at dinner time.

Double or Triple Recipes to Freeze

While I'm not encouraging you to buy frozen foods, I'm all in favor of freezing your own meals. All it takes is some organization; and so many recipes like soups and stews freeze perfectly. You could never tell they've been frozen. It really makes a huge difference. Coming home from a full work day and having something ready is a blessing! Also, plan at least two or three meals at a time, so that your next meal can literally take only ten to fifteen minutes to prepare.

Everything tastes better with *sofrito*

I can't stress enough: everything tastes better with *sofrito*. If you're not familiar with the word, just think of a mixture of garlic, onions, and tomatoes, seasoned with oregano and nutmeg, salt, and pepper. Distribute in little zip-top bags and freeze them. Throw in a sauce, in a stew, in a soup, in quinoa, in wild rice, in just about anything, and flavors will shine bright.

Choose whole grains and whole wheats

You want to choose foods that are as close to their natural state as possible. When flour is refined and processed, most of the nutrients are lost; same with grains. Most grains are composed of three main parts: the germ, the bran, and the endosperm. When eating white rice, for example, we are eating just the endosperm of the grain; brown rice has the full spectrum, along with other rices that are so easy to find, and plenty used in this book, like wild rice or other colored rices.

Make chicken stock at home and freeze

Bear with me! Because this is *the* one ingredient that will change the taste of your cooking forever! I'm not telling you to become a chef, but if there is one item that differentiates restaurant cooking from home cooking, it's chicken stock.

In restaurants, stock is made with bones and aromatic vegetables, then simmered for many hours. Over the years, I tweaked my

method in an attempt to speed up the process. Chicken bones and water. Two ingredients for the home version, and that's it. When I'm in a hurry to make dinner and exhausted from a working day, that's all I can handle.

Especially in recipes like stews, soups, sauces, and even risotto, the quality of a good stock is just phenomenal. My favorite stock is chicken, not only because of the flavor, but because of the gelatin in the bones, which really gives the liquid an amazing texture. Occasionally, I also make vegetable stock or mushroom stock, which are even faster and also full of flavor.

You can make all stocks in big batches and freeze them. When I make chicken stock, I simmer for a good 30 to 45 minutes. But if I'm making vegetable or mushroom stock, I make it on the fly, while chopping onions and a pot of simmering mushroom stock is on for 10 minutes or so. It doesn't need much longer than that.

The technique is easy for all: brown the bones, or vegetables, or mushrooms, making sure to develop crusty bits on the bottom of the pan—that's what's going to give all the flavor to the liquid. Then add cold water, enough to cover the ingredients, bring to a boil, lower the heat, and simmer gently. You never want to boil a stock violently. Low and slow. As simple as it is, there are a few important variables to pay attention to: it's important to occasionally skim off any foam that accumulates on top. Otherwise, your stock could taste slightly bitter. It's also important to strain the liquid really well, using a very fine strainer (or chinois), as the pieces of food left in the liquid will add some impurity if left inside. In the case of chicken stock, I am not too picky if there is a little bit of meat left on the bones, but generally speaking, you want to make sure that the bones are meat-cleaned. The bones are where you'll find all of that precious gelatin and flavor.

Once you start making stock frequently, it gets easier, and your cooking will improve a million points! Like everything in life, it's a matter of habit. This is a good habit that I'd like to preserve, as my cooking certainly benefits from it. Along with my family, and my health.

My Eating Philosophy

Portion Control

In Portuguese, we have a saying: *"Um é pouco, dois é bom, três é demais."* It means, one is too little, two is just right, and three is too much. Words to live by. The American portion sizes are way too big—bigger than any person needs to eat. One way to work around this is to eat meals in a salad plate. A smaller plate will do wonders to help with portion control.

Visit the Local Farmer's Market

It seems so trivial, but in reality, most of the food we buy from a regular supermarket travels an average of fifteen hundred miles from the farm to our plates. Food loses a lot of nutritional value along the way. A local farmer's market will display local foods from local farms that's been picked at the peak of freshness. Plus, it's the best way to discover new ingredients, talk to the vendors, and get ideas for new recipes.

Use Herbs and Spices

In my cooking classes I notice that a lot of people are intimidated to cook with herbs and spices, thinking that there must be a rule of items that go together and make good combinations. The truth is: there are no rules! There are some classics, sure. Mushroom and thyme? Delicious. Pumpkin and cinnamon? Of course! But when it comes to taste, you only need a handful of spices and a few simple techniques for extracting their flavors to surprise and delight your palate. Add spices early in the cooking process, so they have a chance to toast and bloom. Spices are naturally fragrant, but to reach their full flavor potential, if you apply some heat (toasting in a dry pan, or blooming in oil, while cooking garlic and onions) your recipes will taste completely different, a lot deeper, with a profound taste of seasoning. It's a great way to boost flavor in a healthy way. And because there is an abundance of flavor, it reduces the need for more salt.

But pay attention to expiration dates—spices expire in about 1 year or so. If you open a small jar and the aromas don't infuse the air, this means that the spice is going stale. You might want to consider including this in your new year's resolution: clear your spice cabinet; get all new spices and cook with them! The more herbs and spices you use, the more you enhance your diet!

Wake Up: Water Up, Lemon Up, Juice Up!

The moment you wake up is a very important part of your digestion and metabolic system. I've been drinking water, pure lemon juice, and green juices (alternating between these strategies) in the morning for a long time and I find that it helps tremendously to regulate everything, giving me more energy, better cholesterol levels, and helping me maintain a steady weight.

Guide to Superfoods

This section is not a deep study into the life of these amazing superfoods, but rather, a brief highlight of their super powers. Included here are the ones I use most frequently in this book.

Açaí

It almost looks like a blueberry but it grows like a weed on a type of palm tree in the Amazon region. Açaí cannot be eaten raw, only as pulp, which is extracted through the process of maceration. This miracle fruit has one of the highest levels of antioxidants and has long been considered a great anti-aging food. It promotes heart health, aids in weight loss, helps with digestion, improves brain function, and lowers cholesterol levels.

Avocados

One of the first foods associated with Latin cooking. It is also one of the most versatile foods I know, good in savory or sweets, breakfast, lunch, or dinner. It can be the secret to adding creaminess to smoothies, dips, and spreads. Avocados are high in fiber, vitamins, and healthy fats, helping to lower cholesterol and reducing the risks of heart disease.

Beans

Think of edamame, peas, lentils, garbanzo beans, fava beans, lima beans, black beans, and even other dried beans all in the same category. Although they may vary is some characteristics, they all fall under the bean umbrella: plant-based protein. And what a superfood! Beans are a high source of protein, great source of fiber, help regulate blood sugar and cholesterol levels, high in antioxidants and anti-inflammatory.

Bell Peppers, Sweet Peppers, and Hot Peppers

With the explosion of Latin culture and Latin restaurants around the country, the huge variety of peppers that are now available in markets and farm stands is enormous. Peppers come in all different shapes, sizes, and flavors, and there is also a rainbow of sweet and hot peppers out there. You can find way more than the simple (yet delicious) bell peppers; from Cubanelles to poblanos, serrano to arbol. All peppers start out green

and then ripen to the color that they're bred to be. Most peppers varieties are multipurpose. They're good for frying, roasting, sautéing, grilling, pickling, or just eating plain in salads and juices. Select bright, firm peppers with no soft spots or blemishes.

Berries

Açaí, blueberries, strawberries, blackberries, raspberries, and many more, the world of berries is wide and delicious, gorgeous and nutritious. They are high in antioxidants, low in calories, help improve memory and boost brain power; full of fiber; and full of vitamin C.

Brazil Nuts

This nut comes from an enormously tall tree that can reach up to 250 feet in height. Because of its height, the only way to harvest the nuts is to wait for the fruit to fall. In fact, the coconut-like fruit hits the ground with such force after the long drop that it sometimes buries itself in the ground. The nuts that are found inside the fruit capsule are called *ouriço* in Portuguese. These capsules are quite large, about the size of a cantaloupe

melon, and each fruit contains between 10 and 25 nuts. The oblong nut is the part we eat and cook with and has a crunchy yellowish kernel with a very thin brown skin. Brazil nuts are so rich in protein that only 2 nuts are the equivalent of eating an egg. They are also rich in selenium, which protects cells. Store them in the refrigerator or the freezer inside in a zip-lock bag.

Celery

Celery has a silvery green color with powerful characteristics: it is high in vitamin K, which promotes bone and heart health; it has anti-inflammatory effects due to the phytosterol substance that can help with acid reflux, bloating, acne, eczema, and other types of inflammation in the body. It helps with high blood pressure and because it contains bioactive flavonoids, and also helps to fight and prevent cancer cells.

Chayote Squash

Chayote is a tender squash from the same family as melons, cucumbers, and squash. The most common color is a light green vegetable, in the shape of a pear, although darker chayote are starting to appear in Latin markets as well. I'm surprised that chayote isn't already more popular, as the vegetable has great health benefits; it helps regulate cholesterol and helps with weight loss. It's also a rich source of fiber, magnesium, phosphorus, and vitamin C. When handling chayote, the vegetable releases oil that sticks to your hands like wax—which is why often you'll see

them individually wrapped in plastic. I like to wear gloves when handling them.

Chicken and Turkey

It seems almost silly to write about chicken and turkey, since they are some of the most popular, most consumed proteins in this country and around the world. But because there is a large number of recipes in this book devoted to chicken and turkey—as I prepare them often in my American kitchen—let's reserve some attention.

Both chicken and turkey are considered excellent sources of lean protein and highly recommended as part of a healthy diet.

They're rich in vitamins and minerals. Eating poultry helps with the prevention of heart diseases, skin disorders, boosts immunity, and helps prevent diabetes, especially chicken and turkey breasts.

When it comes to buying poultry, generally speaking, whole birds are less expensive (and my preferred way, since I like to use all parts of the bird, especially the bones) than cut-up parts. Today's mass production of bird slaughtering also affects the flavor and quality of its meat. Immediately after slaughtering poultry, birds have to be cooled (according to the USDA, to 40°F) in order to prevent bacteria to grow. The two most common ways of processing birds are water and air chilled. Water chilled means that all birds are submerged in large vats of chlorinated ice water, which lowers the body temperature quickly, but the bird tend to absorb some of the water. Air chilled chicken, on the other hand, takes a little longer to cool the poultry but result in a pure flavor meat as the texture is kept intact. If you don't see any signs of air chilling in the label, assume that chicken was processed in water process.

Chocolate

No, it's not too good to be true: dark chocolate indeed has amazing health benefits. But stick with dark chocolate, please! The compounds that give dark chocolate its bitter flavor are associated with numerous benefits for heart health, blood pressure, and cholesterol levels. Chocolate is also a great source of iron and magnesium. Eat chocolate in moderation, for it's still a very caloric item.

Cocoa nibs (see page 201), are the leftover pieces of processed cocoa beans. Use of these has grown in the cooking world and I love to explore using them in smoothies, breakfast bowls, and for my healthy *brigadeiro*, giving it a delicious crunchy taste. It's chocolate and is healthy! The best quote I've heard about chocolate is: "Chocolate comes from cocoa, which is a tree. That makes it a plant. Chocolate is salad!"

Coconut

The largest nut in the nut world, a whole coconut is the fruit of a coconut palm tree, also called "tree of life" because every part can be used, including the trunk, leaves, husk, and seed. The white flesh is nutty and crunchy and the juice inside—the coconut water—is one of the healthiest liquids you could drink. Countless products come from the coconut and can be used in cooking: coconut water, coconut milk, cream of coconut, coconut oil, coconut flakes, coconut sugar, coconut

flour, and coconut extract. The special type of saturated fat in coconuts is easy to digest and metabolizes as energy. Coconut helps support thyroid function and is rich in magnesium and potassium. It improves digestion, bowel function, immunity, and cholesterol.

Dates

Dates are the fruit of the date palm, a tree that thrives in dry conditions. They are probably the sweetest natural fruit in the world, packed with rich flavors and notes of caramel and toffee. They make a great sugar substitute when added to compotes, quick breads, sauces, or smoothies. Dates are harvested according to stages of ripeness. Choose dates that are plump and glossy. They may look wrinkled, and that's okay, but they should feel soft. Like many dried fruits, dates have a long shelf life and will keep at room temperature for about 2 months if properly sealed in plastic.

Eggplant

This vegetable is of great importance to all types of cuisine, especially Mediterranean and Latin. Its texture is very unique; creamy and meaty, high in fiber and low in calories, which is great for vegetarian and diabetes-friendly recipes. On the other hand, eggplant acts like a sponge and absorbs fats and other liquids, so be conscious about the amount of fat you use when cooking eggplant. Globe eggplant is the easiest to find but you can also use smaller varieties like Japanese, Chinese, and graffiti.

Eggs

Eggs are one of the most complete sources of protein. For some time, eggs were linked to high cholesterol, but more recent studies suggest that the intake of other foods such as carbohydrates can be more impactful on cholesterol levels. Try to buy free-range, organic eggs, meaning that hens were more exposed to sunlight. The brighter the yellow of the yolk, the more nutritional value to the eggs. In terms of shells, the different colors reflect different breed of chickens: brown eggs come from red feather chickens, while white eggs (or sometimes blue-green) come from white feathered chickens. Nutritionally speaking, there isn't a great disparity between the types of eggs.

Fish

If being a delicious and complete source of protein is not enough, here are some more reasons to eat fish: great source of omega-3 fats, nourishes skin and hair, helps reduce

blood pressure and risk of heart attack and stroke, high in quality protein, vitamins B_{12}, D, and many minerals. It's proven that people who eat fish on a regular basis have slower rates of cognitive decline. Fish is really a wonderful food. Try to buy fresh fish, one that smells like the ocean, salty and fresh. Look in the fish's eyes and be sure they are wet and clear. And just like the farmer's market, try to find a fishmonger near you that you trust and know you can get the freshest fish.

Garlic

Some say that garlic is the number 1 healing plant on earth. It is such a powerful effective

food to help fight colds, infections, and improve cardiovascular systems. I just can't live without garlic. In most of my recipes, you'll hear me saying, "cook garlic until it's just golden brown and then add the onions." In my opinion, it changes the flavor profile of everything!

Ginger

Some people love it, some people hate it. Ginger is used in cuisines around the world, and comes in a variety of forms: fresh, pickled, dried, crystalized, and ground. Rarely is ginger used alone in recipes; usually, it's combined with other warm spices, such as cumin, coriander, garlic, turmeric, and many others. Nowadays, ginger can be found in most regular supermarkets, though I still prefer to buy it in Latin or Asian markets. You can keep fresh ginger at room temperature for up to one week, or you can keep it in the fridge for up to one month. Once you cut a piece of fresh ginger from the root, it does not ruin the rest of the root, which make it very practical to always have on hand in the fridge. I like to peel fresh ginger with a paring knife, or you can also use a vegetable peeler.

Hearts of Palm

Palmito in Portuguese, is a vegetable harvested from the inner core of certain palm trees such as *juçara*, *açaí*, and *pejibaye*. It has a nutty, almost artichoke-like flavor, an interesting texture, and it pairs well with an almost endless variety of ingredients. It can be found in regular supermarkets in either a can or a jar, preserved in a citric-acid

solution. In Latin America the most praised kind of *palmito* is the *pupunha*, from yet a fourth kind of palm tree called *pupunheira*, typical in the Amazon region. It is much larger and meatier then the ones we find here in the US.

Hemp, Flax, and Chia Seeds

The use of seeds is growing in the cooking world, as they add flavor and crunch to a variety of recipes, from salads to sweets, juices, and smoothies. These seeds are particularly high in protein, fiber, and omega-3. These heart-healthy fats also help in the prevention of dementia, depression, inflammation, cancer, diabetes, mental decline, and more. Because their oils can go rancid, be sure to store them in the refrigerator or the freezer. You will find plenty of recipes calling for seeds in this book. Feel free to interchange them.

Kale

One of the most nutritional vegetables, kale's popularity has skyrocketed in recent years. It offers a huge dose of vitamin K, more vitamin C than oranges, more calcium than broccoli, and omega-3 fat. And I could go on with more vitamins and minerals, but kale's most impressive quality is the ability to travel to the very center of our cells, empowering our body to clean up and detox. Kale grows well not only during summer time, but also in cold temperatures, so we are able to enjoy it year-round. Its leaves are heartier than other lettuces, which makes it a great idea to marinade kale in salad dressings when eaten raw. But kale is also very versatile, making a great leaf in stews and soups.

Mango

One of the most consumed fruits in the world, and in South America there are more than 1,000 varieties of mango growing today. Mango has a buttery sweet feel, that is both used in sweet and savory dishes. I love to use mango in smoothies and salads. When buying mango, smell it near the stem. It should be fragrant and sweet. When pressing the fruit with your thumb, it should feel slightly soft. Ripen it in paper bag, at room temperature.

Mushrooms

Mushrooms are a great source of fiber, antioxidants, magnesium, and potassium, and are great stimulants to the immune system. There is a wide variety of mushrooms in the market today; many of them are considered to be a delicacy in the cooking world, like shiitake, chanterelles, and especially the famous truffles. In this book, I used mostly shiitake and white button mushrooms, but feel free to upgrade the mushrooms as you wish. When buying mushrooms, choose firm

ones and don't store them in plastic. Keep them in a paper bag in the fridge.

Oranges

Another international fruit and prized in so many cuisines. Navel oranges, Valencia oranges, Seville, blood oranges, and tangerines all make for great juices, marmalades, and snacks. In Latin cooking, as in other types of cuisine, oranges also play a role in savory dishes, showing up in salads (see Orange Salad with Pumpkin Seeds and Crumbled Queso-Blanco on page 93), braises (see Braised Chicken with Fennel and Oranges on page 142) and stews. You will find a wide variety of oranges in the market year-round,

but they're at their peak during the winter months. When choosing oranges, look for a heavy fruit: that's the best indicator of a juicy fruit. You can store oranges at room temperature for a few days, but they will last longer and taste better when refrigerated.

Papayas

Buttery as mangos, papayas came a long way in the past few years and became readily available in most places in the US. Papayas have a smooth green skin that gradually turns yellow as it ripens. The flesh, when ripe and sweet, is salmon-colored, bright orange with a sweet taste to it. Peel the skin, hollow the seeds, and enjoy papayas the same way you would mangos. I love adding papayas to juices, smoothies, and breakfast bowls, as they add a natural creaminess and sweetness that make it irresistible.

Passion Fruit

This fruit is one of my all-time favorites! Its wrinkly skin is an indication of ripeness; the more dimply, the better the flavor. Passion fruit is all about the juice, to the point that you cannot really eat the pulp by itself. Add

a bit of water and pulp into a blender, and force the juice pulp through a strainer, to separate it from the seeds (which are quite crunchy!). The bitter sweet is symbolic of one of the most exotic and delicious tropical fruits!

Peppers, Paprika, and Cayenne

All paprika and cayenne condiments are made from dried chiles and red bell peppers. The two most popular paprika are Hungarian, with a sweet taste and a vibrant red color, and the smoked Spanish paprika, for which the peppers are smoked over an oak fire with a richer taste and end up a darker red. There is a world of small bell peppers (technically, they are a berry fruit) that are interchangeable and used as a condiment. From cayenne, to jalapeno, *malaguetta* or habanero, all these peppers are hot and full of seeds inside.

Pineapple

Pineapple has a bright yellow flesh, with acidity that varies from tart to mild, and complex sweetness. It's used in a variety of recipes in Latin cooking from sweets to salads, salsas, and marinades. When buying pineapple, a good fruit should feel heavy and have a fresh fragrance and give slightly when pressed at the base. A whole pineapple will keep at room temperature for a few days. Once peeled, cored, and cut up, it will last in the fridge for about a week.

Pumpkins

Not to be confused with jack-o-lanterns, the pumpkins I am referring to are the sugar pumpkins, which belong to the squash family, like the butternut squash, acorn squash, and kabocha squash. Their solid texture turns creamy with roasting, steaming, sautéing, or pureeing. Their sweet savory flavor goes well with many baked goods and holiday desserts, just as it does with savory preparations. When buying pumpkins, look for pumpkins that are smaller and rounder, with less defined ridges. You can keep them stored at room temperature for about 3 weeks.

Queso-Blanco

Queso-Blanco is to South America what feta is to Greece, or what mozzarella is to Italy. The taste is also a cross between a feta, a ricotta, and mozzarella. Latinos eat *queso-blanco* in a wide variety of recipes. It's made from cow's milk, and is white, fresh, and firm. Like other fresh white cheeses, *queso-blanco* has a way of complementing other flavors without masking them, and it definitely deserves more attention on its own.

Quinoa

Is quinoa a grain or a seed? Technically it's considered a seed, but for nutrition purposes, it's considered a grain; it originated in South America, most specifically it's indigenous to the Andes in Peru. It can be a great substitute for rice or pasta, but it also makes a great breakfast cereal. It contains a huge amount of protein, fiber, magnesium, B vitamin, and iron. I love everything about quinoa: its taste is lightly nutty and grassy in flavor, with a slight crunch but a soft bite; it cooks quickly, it's convenient, delicious, and healthy. No wonder it became so popular!

Supergreens

Kale was just the beginning. All types of lettuces and leafy vegetables carry boatloads

of nutrients and are very low in calories. In this book, I use many different types of lettuces but feel free to change them up: bok choy, kale, arugula, collard greens, spinach, red leaf lettuce, frisee, escarole, endive, etc.—those are the foods we should mostly be eating, because they're not just greens! They're supergreens!

Sweet Potatoes

Sweet potatoes are originally from South America and are quite similar to yams, which are sweet tubers from Africa and Asia. Although they are not exactly the same, they are completely interchangeable. They are a top source of beta-carotene, which promotes healthy growth, immunity, and vision.

Tomatillo

No, they are *not* green tomatoes! Originated in Mexico and Guatemala, tomatillos are

covered with a waxy green or paper husk and have a very distinct citrusy flavor. It is the key ingredient in many Latin American sauces because it stands up to strong spices, herbs, and chiles. Do not eat tomatillos raw; roasting and boiling them is how you can give them a softer texture and smoother flavor. Before using tomatillos, remove the husks and rinse them in tepid water. Tomatillos are available year-round, and thanks to the popularity of Latin cooking, they're readily available.

Watermelon

This iconic summer fruit has a lot more to offer than what we know. Sure, it's packed with lycopene and vitamins A and C, but more important than that, biting into a fresh piece of sweet and juicy watermelon can make anyone happy. While I still love to eat fresh watermelon, I also love to cook with it, sometimes, preserving its raw state and

adding it to salads and salsas, and other times making juices, granitas, or even grilling watermelon (which really brings out the sweetness). Because of its size, it very common to see a half watermelon for sale and that's okay, as the fruit doesn't go bad too fast after it's cut. There are tons of varieties of watermelon, but what we see most commonly in the markets are the icebox and picnic watermelon, averaging about 10 to 30 pounds per fruit. I also like the mini, or seedless, watermelon, with a more delicate rind. Even yellow watermelon can be found these days and they are interchangeable. Feel free to play and explore with this delicious fruit.

Yucca

This root vegetable has many names: cassava and yucca in English and Spanish; *aipim*, *mandioca*, and *macaxeira* in Portuguese. Yucca is a perennial shrub with slender leaves and a cluster of roots that grows in the ground. Most of the yucca found in Latin markets in the US comes from Costa Rica or the Dominican Republican and is coated with a thin wax to protect the vegetable. Though unfortunately, this waxing is not always a foolproof method, so I've learned the hard way to always buy more yucca than the recipe calls for, in case there are any bad roots.

Of all tuber vegetables, yucca is the highest yielding crop and sometimes, it can remain unharvested for up to 2–3 years, gaining in starch content. Speaking of starch, this the central appeal of yucca; several by-products resulting from pressing the yucca starch are extracted as a fine white powder and used in cooking around the world. In recent years, as the crave for gluten-free products keeps growing, manioc starch is one of the most common substitutes for wheat flour. Let's talk about them:

Manioc Flour or Manioc Meal

In Latin America, yucca meal and starch are used in a variety of recipes and preparations from bread rolls to crackers, doughs, crepes, and fritters. In Brazil, yucca meal is used as a side dish (*farinha de mandioca* in Portuguese) and served with soups, stews, and rice and beans. Manioc flour is a staple pantry ingredient with a long shelf life. The vegetable is ground in a food processor, squeezed in a cheesecloth to remove any liquid, pressed into a tight block, and wrapped again in cheesecloth. It sits at room temperature with bricks on top for 24 hours. The next day, the vegetable is unwrapped, sifted, and spread in a flat tray to air-dry for another 24 hours. The following day, it is lightly toasted on a skillet over low heat.

Manioc Starch

Manioc starch (*harina de yuca* in Spanish; *povilho doce* in Portuguese) and sour manioc starch (*povilho azedo*) are both extracted from yucca. The vegetable is first grated and washed, and its pulp is squeezed over a bucket. The starch accumulated in the bucket is then separated from the liquid, which is then dried and sifted. The difference between them is a natural fermentation process undergone by the sour starch when it is left to sit at room temperature for a period of 15 days to ferment. The manioc starch has a much finer consistency and more delicate texture than the sour manioc starch and is mostly used in sweets and crackers.

Although it may sound a little confusing, don't mistake manioc starch for manioc flour. It gets even more confusing because in English, manioc starch is usually called tapioca flour.

So let's lay out a few terms used in this book with quick translations:

Manioc flour = manioc meal = *farinha de mandioca* (used to make *farofa*, see page 2 and page 185)

Povilho doce = manioc starch = tapioca flour (used to make *pao de queijo* and other baked goods)

Povilho azedo = fermented sour manioc starch = fermented tapioca flour (used to make Gluten-Free Cheese Crackers on page 65); no American brand makes the equivalent of the sour manioc starch. So for recipes in this book calling for povilho azedo, I recommend buying the product in Latin markets or online (Amafil and Yoki are the most popular brands).

Flavored Waters, Juices, Smoothies & Bowls

Minty Lemony Agua Fresca   29

Orange Fennel Agua Fresca   29

Sunny Smoothie   31

Bluebie Orange Smoothie   31

Carrot Ginger Smoothie   32

Cucumba Lemonade   33

Papa Coco Cash Bowl   34

Be My Date Bowl   35

Açaí Power Bowl   37

Survivor Bowl   39

Mango Lassi   39

Pumpkin Protein Shake   41

Brazil Nut Latte   41

Tropical Granola   43

Minty Lemony Agua Fresca

Eat a cucumber! And drink one, too! This is how I say summer. I love using coconut water when making flavored waters, but feel free to use plain water. **Makes 2 (16 oz. each) jars**

6 sprigs fresh mint
10 thin slices cucumber
1 lime, sliced thinly
4 cups coconut water
Ice cubes

1. Divide the mint, cucumber, and lime between 2 mason jars. Fill each with coconut water. Close the jar and let it steep in the fridge for at least 2 hours or overnight. Add ice before serving.

Orange Fennel Agua Fresca

Let's take a cue from Latin água fresca and go for the glow! Think of this water as your personal cleansing drink. As in, hello health! All you need is a few sips to brighten your daytime energy. **Makes 1 (16 oz.) mason jar**

3–4 thin slices navel orange
1 stalk fennel plus fennel top, cut into chunks
2 cups coconut water
Ice cubes

1. Combine the orange slices, fennel, and coconut water in a mason jar. Close the jar and let it steep in the fridge for at least 2 hours or overnight. Add ice before serving.

Sunny Smoothie

A recipe that has earned its place in the sun. Recently the surge of papayas in the market brings me right back home. When I come back from the gym, I can make this in less than 5 minutes. **Makes 1 drink**

½ cup cubed papaya
⅓ cup fresh orange juice
   (about 1 navel orange)
½ cup fresh tangerine juice
   (about 1 tangerine)
½ cup coconut water

1. Put everything in a blender and blend for 2 minutes until completely smooth. Pour into a tall glass and serve immediately.

Bluebie Orange Smoothie

You leave the house at 7:00 a.m. and come home, exhausted, at 7:00 p.m. All family members are engaged in other activities and dinner is not required that night. You're just too tired to cook. But you still want to prepare something healthy, homemade. Kitchen meets dinner, right here. This recipe gets that. Make it double and breakfast is ready. **Makes 1 drink**

1 cup blueberries
½ cup orange juice
½ cup coconut water
½ cup ice cubes

1. Put everything in a blender and blend for 2 minutes until completely smooth. Pour into a tall glass and serve immediately.

Carrot Ginger Smoothie

This recipe is to inspire you to declare your allegiance to healthy cooking via a simple smoothie and prove that one's kitchen should be the ultimate expression of its family's beliefs. **Makes 2 smoothies**

3 carrots, juiced
   (about ⅓ cup juice)
1 tsp. ginger, juiced
½ orange bell pepper, juiced
   (about ⅓ cup juice)
1 cup cubed cantaloupe
⅓ cup crushed ice

1. Combine the juices of carrot, ginger, and orange bell pepper with the cantaloupe and crushed ice. Combine well in a blender until homogeneous.

Cucumba Lemonade

This is the drink of my hopes. It fills my heart with joy of health, and makes me happy to feel healthy.
Makes 1 Drink

1 English cucumber, peeled and seeded
4–5 sprigs dill
2 tablespoons fresh lemon juice
$\frac{1}{2}$ cup coconut water

1. In a juice extractor, press the juice of the cucumber and dill; you should have about $\frac{2}{3}$ cup. Transfer to a blender with the lemon juice and coconut water, and pulse together. Pour into a glass and serve.

Papa Coco Cash Bowl
(Papaya, Coconut, Cashew)

If eating a papaya is the closest you've ever been to South America, this recipe brings it to the next level. The Latin colors, flavors, and textures are worked in this Papaya Coconut Cashew Bowl, and make you want to bring sunlight to your heart. **Makes 1 serving**

For the Bowl:
1 full cup papaya, cut into cubes
8 dried apricots, soaked in hot water for 5 minutes
¼ cup cashew butter
1 banana, sliced (reserve ¼ for garnish)
¼ cup coconut milk
½ cup crushed ice

For the Garnish:
¼ sliced banana
2 tablespoons unsweetened coconut, lightly toasted
1 tablespoon cashews, roughly chopped
2 teaspoons chia seeds

1. Place in a blender the papaya, soaked apricots, cashew butter, ¾ of a banana, coconut milk, and the crushed ice.

2. Blend well until it's the consistency of a thick pudding.

3. Pour into a bowl, and garnish with more banana, coconut, cashews, and chia seeds. Serve immediately.

Be My Date Bowl

Cheers to my daughter Bianca, who started eating smoothie bowls after cheerleading practice. Cheerleading? This sport doesn't even exist in Latin America! I had to learn so much about American culture and my kids are my greatest teachers. I've been living in the US close to 20 years, but forever will remain a fiery Latina! I am her date in eating this bowl. This smoothie bowl can be breakfast, lunch, or dinner, and will boost your superpowers. Make it once, follow the recipe; make it twice, feel free to explore and use this as a guideline. Smoothie bowls are one of my favorite meals! **Makes 2 medium bowls or 1 large**

For the Bowl:

2 bananas
¼ cup almond milk
3 dates, pitted and roughly chopped
⅓ cup almond butter
¼ teaspoon cocoa powder
¼ teaspoon cinnamon
¼ teaspoon vanilla extract (optional)
¾ cup crushed ice

For the Garnish:

¼ cup fresh blueberries
¼ cup almond granola

1. Peel and chop roughly 1½ bananas. Save the other half for garnish.

2. Combine the banana, almond milk, dates, almond butter, cocoa powder, cinnamon, and vanilla extract in a blender. Start on slow speed and gradually increase. Once everything is well pureed, add the crushed ice and blend on low speed until the consistency of the mixture resembles a pancake batter.

3. Pour into a bowl and garnish with the remaining ½ banana, cut into thin rounds, blueberries, and granola. Serve immediately.

Açaí Power Bowl

Rio de Janeiro: *Amidst its fame for samba, carnival, and beaches, a curious girl with a passion for food was born. A natural playground for music, cooking, and happiness, it's also home to some of the most spectacular farmer's markets in the world. I go back home often to visit my roots, and the more I visit, the more I am in awe of our culture. This recipe is a tribute to the açaí bowls I grew up eating in the streets of Rio.* **Makes 1 bowl**

For the Bowl:
2 bananas
½ cup açaí frozen pulp, thawed
¼ cup almond milk
¼ cup almond butter
2 teaspoons cocoa powder
½ cup crushed ice

For the Garnish:
½ banana, sliced
1 tablespoon cacao nibs
2 tablespoons granola

1. Peel and chop roughly 2 bananas.

2. Combine the banana, açaí, almond milk, almond butter, and cocoa powder in a blender. Start on slow speed and gradually increase. Once everything is pureed, add the crushed ice and blend on low speed until the consistency of the mixture is just below a pudding.

3. Pour into a bowl and garnish with sliced banana, cacao nibs, and granola. Serve immediately.

Survivor Bowl

These embellished bowls have become a regular in my kitchen. They make a statement when bejeweled with granolas, fruits, and seeds. Feel free to change cashew butter for almond butter. I make it often after I take a "survivor" spinning class. **Makes 1 large bowl, or 2 small bowls**

For the Bowl:
1/3 cup almond butter
1 cup spinach leaves
1/4 teaspoon cinnamon
1/4 cup coconut milk
1/2 teaspoon matcha powder
1 1/2 bananas, chopped
1/2 cup crushed ice

For the Garnish:
1/2 banana, thinly sliced
2 tablespoons granola
1 tablespoon hulled hemp seeds

1. Place almond butter, spinach, cinnamon, coconut milk, and matcha powder in the bowl of a blender and puree until smooth.

2. Add bananas, along with 1/2 cup crushed ice. Blend well.

3. Carefully pour into a large bowl.

4. Garnish with banana slices, granola, and hemp seeds. Serve immediately.

Mango Lassi

I love Indian food, especially because there are plenty of similarities between Latin and Asian ingredients. Mangoes, for example—a tropical fruit in Latin cooking, a basic fruit to Indian cuisine. Mango Lassi is a classic Indian drink that's easy to make at home. Here I've prepared a lighter version with almond milk. A little ground cardamom sprinkled on top and you can touch the sky! **Makes 1 tall glass**

1 cup diced ripe mango
3/4 cup almond milk
1 teaspoon honey
A few drops lime juice
1/2 cup crushed ice
1/4 teaspoon ground cardamom
1/4 teaspoon lime zest

1. Combine the mango, almond milk, honey, lime juice, and ice in a blender and puree until smooth. Taste and add a bit more milk if it's too thick. Sprinkle some ground cardamom and lime zest. Pour into a tall glass and serve.

Note: You can use either fresh mango (my preference), frozen mango chunks, or frozen mango pulp. If you use fresh, you'll want to use a ripe, sweet mango.

Pumpkin Protein Shake

Some ingredients were simply made for each other. To wit: pumpkin and coconut; although not quite opposite in textures, they certainly attract in Latin lands. You can find this combination in a variety of cooking and baking items as it offers a thoughtful balance of sweetness and nutty earth flavors. In my unstoppable work to inspire people to cook more and more at home, this protein shake brings health, vigor, and energy. Perfect for after jogging! **Makes 2 tall shakes**

1 cup coconut milk (or almond milk)
½ cup canned pumpkin puree
1 banana, peeled and roughly sliced
1 tablespoon peanut butter
½ teaspoon honey
½ cup crushed ice

1. Place everything in a blender and beat well until light and frothy. Pour into tall glasses, and garnish with a dust of cinnamon. Serve immediately.

Brazil Nut Latte

In Latin America the practice of grinding nuts and turning them into milk drinks, called horchata, dates back from Spanish colonization. Today, horchata is all over (just not with this name) and if you think that the trendy soy and almond milk are the only options for alternative milks, Brazil nuts make a great addition to that category! For those who are lactose intolerant, this recipe is just perfect, delicious, and super nutritional. Like most nuts, Brazil nuts are full of vitamins and minerals. They have good fats and lots of protein. Two Brazil nuts have the equivalent protein of one egg! So, if you want some samba across your tongue, you'll have it with this Brazil Nut Latte! **Serves 4 to 6**

½ pound Brazil nuts
4 cups water
1 teaspoon vanilla extract
1 teaspoon ginger, finely minced or grated
½ teaspoon cinnamon
3 tablespoons maple syrup

1. In a high-speed blender, blend all the ingredients until smooth.

2. Strain through a fine sieve and serve very cold.

Tropical Granola

Granola is associated with healthy foods all over the world, and Latin America is not any different. For many years, I used to buy granola from the store, until the day I decided to make it myself; not only I have much better control of what goes inside, it's also a lot cheaper. Of course, I could never make a granola not using my beloved tropical nuts; I developed this recipe a few years ago and have been making big batches about once a month. I put it in a large glass container, and it stays fresh for the whole month at room temperature. It also makes a terrific food gift! **Makes 8 cups (or about 4 tall mason jars)**

3 cups old fashioned rolled oats

½ cup chopped Brazil nuts

½ cup cashews

1 cup dried, shredded, unsweetened coconut

¼ cup sunflower seeds

¼ cup pumpkin seeds

½ cup light brown sugar

1 teaspoon kosher salt

½ teaspoon cinnamon

½ teaspoon freshly ground nutmeg

½ cup olive oil

½ cup honey

1 teaspoon vanilla extract

2 egg whites, lightly beaten with a fork

¾ cup chopped dried fruit (raisins, apricots, banana chips)

1. Preheat the oven to 275°F.

2. In a large bowl, mix the oats, nuts, coconut, seeds, sugar, salt, cinnamon, and nutmeg. Make sure there are no lumps of brown sugar.

3. In another small bowl, whisk together the oil, honey, and vanilla. Pour the liquid mixture into the dry mixture and fold well with a rubber spatula, making sure every oat and nut is covered.

4. Add the egg whites and fold everything together. Pour and spread the mixture onto a half sheet pan lined with silicone mat and bake for about 45 to 60 minutes, or until the mixture is medium brown and toasty. Stir every 20 minutes, moving the crispy bits from the perimeter into the center and distributing the granola in the center out toward the edge of the pan.

5. Remove the pan from the oven and immediately add the dried fruit. Using a spatula, stir to combine the mixture and let the granola cool. The mixture will be sticky when it comes out of the oven but will dry out as it cools. Transfer to a large mason jar container. It will stay fresh for up to one month.

Appetizers

Brazilian Guacamole 47

Gorgonzola Mousse 49

Hearts of Palm and Spinach Dip 50

Tortilla Espanola 51

Tapioca Crepe with Tomato Mozzarella 55

Salmon Marinated in Celery Juice 57

Tequila Gravlax 59

Scrambled Eggs with Romesco Sauce 60

Spinach Minas Quiche 62

Gluten-Free Cheese Crackers 65

Hearts of Palm Ceviche 67

Huevos Cubanos 69

Spinach Mushroom Quesadilla 71

Ceviche with Tiger's Milk 73

Kale Gnocchi 74

Watercress Flan 76

Brazilian Guacamole

Maybe it will happen during a soccer match. Or maybe it will happen later on, during a sports game, or next year's Super Bowl. But at some point, you are likely to have a bunch of friends come over for a party or BBQ. Chances of guacamole being on the menu are high. And if you like guacamole, you will love this recipe; it's my take on the Mexican dish. It's similar in the sense that is an avocado dip served with chips—it's different because it has all the colors of the rainbow. Make your kitchen guac again! **Makes 3½ cups; serves 8 to 10 people**

1 clove garlic, finely minced
2 scallions, chopped
Half red onion, finely chopped
Half red bell pepper, finely
    diced
Half yellow bell pepper, finely
    diced
Half an english cucumber,
    peeled, seeded, and finely
    diced
1 plum tomato, peeled,
    seeded, and finely diced
1 tablespoon soy sauce
1 teaspoon salt and freshly
    ground black pepper
¼ cup chopped fresh parsley
¼ cup chopped fresh cilantro
2 ripe Hass avocados
¼ cup extra-virgin olive oil

1. Combine the garlic, scallions, red onion, bell peppers, cucumber, and tomato, and toss well.

2. Season with the soy sauce, salt and pepper, parsley, and cilantro, and fold well.

3. Cut the avocados in half, remove the pits, and scoop the flesh out of their shells. Dice to about the same size as the other ingredients and add to the bowl.

4. Slowly pour the olive oil and fold everything carefully. Taste again to check seasoning. Refrigerate for at least 3 hours so that flavors can develop but remove from the fridge at least 20 minutes before serving. Serve with toasts and/or crackers.

Salmon Marinated in Celery Juice

In the big leagues of French cuisine, there is one chef who has consistently challenged the potential of salmon, and he's done it with a knife, salt, pepper, olive oil, and his French accent. His name is Jacques Pepin. When I was in cooking school, I went to many demos from the master, always sitting in the first row, and writing just about every word out of his mouth. Looking back, I realize those demos gave me wings to fly, and over the years, I started exploring ways to use salmon in a variety of recipes. For lovers of sushi and sashimi, this dish presents a jazzy approach. It has all of the qualities of a sushi/sashimi dish, without the rice. Here, the fish is not only marinated, but perfumed in the delicate aromas of celery and ginger, creating a silky texture. You can use any part of salmon, but it's best if you use a portion from the center cut. Sometimes the most mundane ingredients are the ones that become the object of desire! **Serves 4**

For the Salmon:
¼ pound salmon, center cut, skinless
Kosher salt and freshly ground pepper
3 tablespoons olive oil

For the Marinade:
½ cup celery juice (from 2 stalks)
1 tablespoon ginger juice (from 3 ounces)
1 teaspoon lemon zest
½ cup freshly chopped dill
1 teaspoon "Sprinkling Yuzu" (or substitute with a mix of white and black sesame seeds)

1. Use a long, thin bladed knife to cut the salmon into thin slices, about ⅛- to ¼-inch thick. Arrange them nicely on a large platter with a rim. Season with salt and pepper, and drizzle olive oil all over the salmon.

2. Mix the celery and ginger juice and pour carefully over the salmon.

3. Garnish with the lemon zest, dill, and Sprinkling Yuzu. Let the salmon marinade for 10 to 15 minutes before serving.

Tequila Gravlax

Say Tequila! Say Salmon! Then raise a glass! Vacuum-sealed packages of smoked salmon are easy to find in a regular supermarket and can last up to three weeks in the refrigerator. That said, most often I find them to be either too dry, or too salty, or too thick. In my opinion, the perfect smoked salmon should be oily (but not too much), salty (but not too much), and it needs to be sliced paper-thin right before eating, almost translucent. I don't have a smoker in my house, so I often satisfy my cravings for smoked salmon with its cousin gravlax, with a Latin twist, of course.

Gravlax is a Scandinavian style salmon turned universal, in which the fish is cured in a mixture of salt and sugar, seasoned with herbs (and spices if you want) and a little alcohol. The name comes from the Swedish word gravid (buried) and lax (salmon). This is really a miracle cure: the salt sucks up the moisture causing the fish to toughen up. Salt is also a great preserver and gravlax can stay in the fridge for a long time.

A lot of people don't venture into making gravlax, but if you give a try, you'll be shocked at how simple this is. I love it for so many reasons: it's lean and healthy, easy to prepare, and it lasts a long time. Not to mention that it makes for a very elegant appetizer. **Serves 4 to 6**

1¼ pound salmon fillet, skin on
½ cup freshly chopped cilantro
½ cup freshly chopped dill
⅓ cup kosher salt
½ cup organic cane sugar
1 teaspoon freshly ground black pepper
4 tablespoons tequila

1. Make sure the salmon is free of any bones. If you see any, remove them with tweezers. Cut a few strips through the salmon skin, being careful not to cut too deep.

2. In a bowl, mix together the herbs, salt, sugar, pepper, and tequila.

3. Place the salmon skin side down in a baking dish large enough to hold the salmon. Pour half of the mixture on the bottom of the fish and half of the mixture on top, massaging well and making sure every single space of salmon is covered in the cure. Wrap the dish tightly in plastic film and refrigerate for a minimum of 24 hours, preferably 2 days, turning the fish every 12 hours.

4. When ready to serve, wipe the dill mixture from the salmon and rinse the fish in cold running water. Pat dry.

5. Use a long and thin knife to slice the salmon and make paper-thin slices, arranging on a platter. Serve with crackers, or toast, or pumpernickel bread.

Scrambled Eggs with Romesco Sauce

Magic in the world of food often happens using whatever ingredients you have on hand. Got eggs? Then let's make some magic. This recipe is inspired by a Spanish dish I ate at a New York City restaurant called Gato, from legendary chef Bobby Flay. It's probably one of the most profitable restaurant dishes considering the ingredients are fairly inexpensive, and one of the fastest if you consider the menu for a family dinner. Whether in a restaurant kitchen or in your home kitchen, the most important aspect is that this recipe honors foods that bring passion and flavor to reinventing the essentials, and making everyday recipes taste magical. Once you prepare the Romesco sauce (which you can prepare and freeze in portions), this recipe takes all of 2 minutes. I am looking forward to having you cook this recipe at home; you'll never think of scrambled eggs the same way again! **Serves 2**

1 teaspoon butter

1 teaspoon olive oil

4 eggs, at room temperature

2 tablespoons heavy cream

Kosher salt and freshly ground
    pepper

2 tablespoons Romesco sauce

1 tablespoon Boucheron
    cheese, cut into small
    pieces

2 tablespoons freshly
    chopped parsley

1 teaspoon finely chopped and
    crushed almonds

Drizzle of olive oil for garnish

1. Put a large nonstick sauté pan over medium heat and add the butter and oil.

2. In a medium bowl, beat the eggs and heavy cream with a pinch of salt and pepper.

3. Add the eggs to the pan, turn down the heat to medium-low, and mix with a wooden spoon, continuously but gently scraping the base and sides of the pan.

4. Add the Romesco sauce, Boucheron cheese, and half of the parsley and continue mixing, working really fast not to dry out the eggs. You will be cooking the eggs for a total of 2 to 3 minutes—that's it! Transfer to a medium bowl, and garnish with the remaining parsley, almonds, and olive oil. Serve immediately.

Romesco Sauce

Makes about 2 cups

2 bread slices, crust removed, torn into pieces

1 cup blanched almonds, lightly toasted

1 clove garlic

1 cup fresh parsley leaves

2 red bell peppers, roasted, skinned, seeded, and roughly chopped (or you can use jarred red bell pepper)

1 plum tomato, skinned, seeded, and roughly chopped

1 teaspoon red wine vinegar

2 teaspoons Spanish paprika

Kosher salt and freshly ground pepper

$\frac{1}{2}$ cup olive oil

1. Place the bread, nuts, garlic, and parsley in a food processor and beat until finely ground. It should look like sand at this point.

2. Add the roasted pepper, tomato, vinegar, paprika, salt, and pepper, and beat some more, scraping the sides of the bowl.

3. With the machine running, add the olive oil in a steady stream and beat until well combined. Taste and adjust the seasoning. Store in jars in the refrigerator up to 2 weeks, or you can keep in smaller containers in the freezer and use as needed.

Spinach Minas Quiche

Brunch doesn't exist in Portuguese or Spanish. Neither the word, nor the tradition. In Latin America, the habit of combining lunch and dinner is quite more usual than combining breakfast and lunch. For this, I often make quiche! This one is especially delicious, using spinach and Minas cheese, or queso blanco. It's a thoughtful balance, and then, boom! The unexpected wins out. Usually when I eat spinach quiche, there is a bare trace of spinach and the rest is big chunks of custard. Not here. This recipe is more than fantastic; it's loaded with greens and packed with flavors; the custard comes in just to bind everything. A recipe to cook often. A recipe to hold on to. **Serves 8**

For the Tart Dough:
1¹⁄₃ cups all-purpose flour
Pinch salt
½ cup cold unsalted butter, cut into cubes
4 tablespoons cold water

For the Quiche:
1 tablespoon olive oil
3 cloves garlic, finely mashed
10 ounces washed and dried fresh spinach
Kosher salt and freshly ground pepper
1 shallot, finely minced
7 ounces Minas cheese, cut into small cubes (or queso blanco, or any other white fresh cheese)
3 eggs
1 cup fat-free milk
2 tablespoons Parmesan cheese
Pinch of freshly grated nutmeg
Tiny pinch paprika

Equipment: 9-inch round pie dish or quiche pan; pie weights or dried beans

1. **Make the Tart Dough**: in a food processor combine the flour and a pinch of salt. Pulse to mix. Add the butter and pulse until it looks like sand. Turn the machine on and carefully add the cold water just until the dough starts forming a ball. Transfer to a floured work surface, shape into a flat disk, and wrap it in plastic film. Chill for at least 30 minutes. Dough can be prepared up to 5 days ahead of time and kept in the fridge or frozen up to 1 month.

2. Preheat the oven to 365°F. On a floured surface, roll out the dough into a round disk about 10 inches in diameter, or a few inches larger than the size of your mold. Carefully transfer to the quiche pan. Press the dough into the bottom and sides of the pan. Pinch the dough around the rim to form a fluted edge.

3. Line the dough with foil and fill with pie weights or dried beans. Bake until the crust is dry, about 15 minutes. Remove from the oven and lift the beans and parchment paper. Reduce the oven temperature to 350°F. Return the dough to the oven and bake again until the dough is lightly golden brown, another 10 minutes. Transfer to a wire rack and cool completely.

4. **Prepare the Spinach:** While the pie crust is baking, warm the olive oil in a large pan. Add the garlic and cook until it just starts to turn golden, about 2 minutes.

5. Add the spinach all at once, and mixing with a pair of tongs, mix the spinach with the garlic. It will wilt quite fast. Season

with salt and pepper and continue cooking. Add the shallot and mix everything together. Taste the spinach and make sure it's well seasoned. Transfer to a plate and let it cool completely. Once cool, transfer to a cutting board, and chop the spinach. Transfer to a bowl and mix with the cubed Minas cheese.

6. In another bowl, mix the eggs, milk, and Parmesan together until well blended. Season with salt, pepper, nutmeg, and a little bit of paprika.

7. Arrange the spinach and cheese mixture over the cooled crust. Slowly pour the egg mixture over the spinach-cheese mixture.

8. Carefully transfer to the oven and bake on the center rack until the top is lightly browned and the filling is just set, about 40 to 45 minutes. If the center of the quiche is still a little wabbly when you remove from the oven, bake for another 5 minutes until it's set. Transfer to a wire rack and let it cool for 10 minutes before serving. Cut into wedges and serve warm.

Gluten-Free Cheese Crackers

Here is a yucca starch-based cheese cracker that's easy to prepare and quite delicious to snack. It's a cousin of Pão de Queijo (the iconic Brazilian cheese bread); the recipe calls for manioc starch and cheese as its main ingredients. The difference, however, is that Pão de Queijo is more of a bread roll—chewy, steamy, almost succulent, while this recipe resembles more of a cheese cracker. The manioc starch gives the cracker a melt-in-your-mouth feel that's absolutely irresistible, increasing that razor flakiness, toasty flavor, and golden looks. Once you get the hang of it, which you should be able to do after a single try, play around a bit. You might want to change the shape, or even add spices. Some paprika and nutmeg would be nice. Swapping Parmesan for Pecorino is okay too. **Makes about 30 crackers**

1 stick unsalted butter, cut into cubes, at room temperature

1 cup *povilho azedo* (sour manioc starch)

1 teaspoon salt

1 large egg

1 cup freshly grated Parmesan cheese

1. Preheat the oven to 350°F. Line a baking sheet with parchment paper or silicone mat.

2. In the bowl of an electric mixer fitted with the paddle attachment, beat the butter, manioc, and salt on medium speed until light and creamy, about 2 minutes. Add the egg and continue to beat, scraping the sides of the bowl as needed, until the dough is well kneaded, about 2 minutes. Add the cheese and mix well.

3. Using a tablespoon, scoop the dough into little balls and work them in your hands into a strip about 3 inches long. Using a fork or the dull side of a knife, score the dough lightly 2 to 3 times, and shape the dough into a little crescent circle, pinching them at the ends. Repeat the process with all the dough.

4. Space the crackers 1 inch apart on the prepared baking sheet. Bake, rotating the sheet once halfway through, until they are lightly golden brown, about 12 minutes. Remove the baking sheet from the oven and transfer the crackers to a wire rack. Let them cool completely and serve. Crackers can be kept in an airtight container at room temperature for up to 5 days. If you would like to eat them extra crunchy, reheat them in a 300°F oven for 4 minutes before serving.

Hearts of Palm Ceviche

Shop local, eat global. These days, you don't have to go to a Latin market to make good Latin food—most major supermarkets carry the basics in their international aisles. Add hearts of palm to the list of basics, for sure. This is a fun play on ceviche—vegan style, plant based. Light on your stomach; heavy on taste and deliciousness. Invite some friends over for Saturday night, set a nice table, and have a great time! **Serves 4**

2 (14-ounce) cans hearts of palm (I used Goya)

2 tablespoons freshly squeezed lime juice (about 1 lime)

$1/4$ cup finely chopped red bell pepper

$1/4$ cup finely chopped yellow bell pepper

$1/4$ cup finely chopped green bell pepper

1 plum tomato, peeled, seeded, and finely chopped

$1/4$ cup finely chopped red onions

Kosher salt and freshly ground pepper

$1/4$ cup extra-virgin olive oil

3 tablespoons freshly chopped cilantro

3 tablespoons freshly chopped mint

1. Drain the hearts of palm and wash them in cold water. Let them dry in a colander for 5 minutes, then slice them into $1/2$-inch thick coins. All together you should have $2^3/4$ cups hearts of palm slices. Place them in a large bowl.

2. Add the lime juice, bell peppers, tomato, and red onion. Season lightly with salt and pepper.

3. Add the olive oil and fold everything together.

4. Add the herbs and mix, folding carefully to maintain the hearts of palm whole. Divide the ceviche among 4 small beautiful glasses or small plates, garnish with some microgreens or whatever herbs you have handy, and serve immediately.

Note About Hearts of Palm: Hearts of palm comes from the trunk of palm trees. With delicate flavors and mild texture, this vegetable is similar in taste and use to asparagus and artichokes. It's great in salads, soups, and braised dishes. In the US, the most common type of hearts of palm is found in cans or jars, and these days you can find them just about anywhere. If you are really looking for fresh hearts of palm though—and I highly recommend trying it sometime—you can try melissas. com. In steak houses all over South America, I urge you to try the "Palmito Pupunha," which is a fresh thick trunk of palm, served grilled. It's so delicious and different! Costa Rica and Brazil are the biggest producers of hearts of palm.

Huevos Cubanos

While this classic dish is all over Latin America, it's most prominent in Cuba, called Huevos Cubanos, and in Mexico, called Huevos Rancheros. What I love about this dish is that it's packed with flavor from the bell peppers, tomatoes, herbs, and spices. It's also high in protein! It can be served family style, or in individual dishes. It's also quite versatile: it can be served for breakfast, lunch, or dinner. You can either prepare in a baking dish in the oven, or you can prepare the recipe using a pan and cook it right on the stove top. The vegetables can be prepared ahead of time, making life very practical. Isn't this what we all want? **Serves 4**

2 tablespoons olive oil

2 cloves garlic, finely minced

1 red onion, chopped finely

½ green bell pepper, seeded and diced

½ yellow bell pepper, seeded and diced

2 plum tomatoes, peeled, seeded, and diced

Kosher salt and freshly ground pepper

Pinch of paprika

Freshly ground nutmeg

¼ cup chicken stock

2 tablespoons fresh chopped parsley, more for topping

4 eggs

Equipment: 7 x 11 baking dish, lightly greased with cooking spray

1. Preheat the oven to 350°F.

2. In a large nonstick skillet, warm the oil over low heat. Add the garlic and cook until it just starts to turn golden, about 1 minute.

3. Add the onion and bell peppers and cook, stirring frequently with a wooden spoon until nice and translucent, about 3 minutes. If the vegetables start to burn, add a splash of water or chicken stock.

4. Add the tomatoes and cook until they start to release their juices and get mushy, about 2 minutes. Season with salt, pepper, paprika, and nutmeg.

5. Add the chicken stock and continue cooking until the mixture looks moist but not liquid, about 3 minutes. Add the parsley and mix well.

6. Carefully pour the mixture into the baking dish and spread evenly with a spatula. Using the spatula, push vegetables around to create 4 "holes" and break the eggs, one at a time, into each space. Season eggs with salt and pepper. Bake, uncovered, until the eggs are done to your liking, about 10 minutes for soft with a runny yolk, or an additional 5 minutes for a hard-cooked egg. Let it sit for 5 minutes before serving. Garnish with parsley on top.

Spinach Mushroom Quesadilla

Certain dishes have their own versions in every type of international cuisine. I'd say that quesadilla is the Mexican version of grilled cheese sandwich. In Brazil, we have the Misto Quente, which is similar to the American version, made with bread, cheese, and a slice of turkey or ham. In Mexico, quesadillas are prepared most often with corn tortillas; in the US, flour tortillas are more common, which I must say works very well because the flour tortilla crisps up quite well in a skillet or griddle and retains the heat better than the corn tortilla.

When it comes to filling, you can put just about any melting cheese and your quesadilla will be wonderful. In the light of keeping things healthy, I often stick to fresh mozzarella, which has a beautiful melting factor, or queso-blanco, but virtually any melting cheese works fine. The mushroom-spinach quesadilla with mozzarella is a simple combination that works beautiful; I like to cut into wedges and serve as a pass-around starters for a family meal. Another extra point is that quesadilla is one of those dishes that can be eaten as breakfast, lunch, or dinner. My kids love it! **Makes 4 quesadillas**

3 tablespoons olive oil

8 ounces cremini mushrooms, stems removed, sliced

Kosher salt and freshly ground pepper

Freshly ground nutmeg

½ small shallot, finely minced

1 clove garlic, minced

6 ounces baby spinach (about 5 cups)

4 whole wheat tortillas

1 cup fresh white mozzarella or queso-blanco

Dried oregano, for garnish

1. In a medium skillet, warm 1 tablespoon of the olive oil over high heat and add the mushrooms. Cook, stirring frequently, until they start to release their water, about 4 minutes. Season with salt, pepper, and nutmeg, and add the shallot. Taste and adjust the seasoning. Cook for another minute and transfer to a plate. Let it cool completely.

2. Wipe the pan and add the remaining 2 tablespoons olive oil. Add the garlic and cook until it just starts to turn golden, about 1 minute. Add the spinach and cook, stirring vigorously, until it wilts completely, about 3 minutes. Season with salt, pepper, and nutmeg. Transfer to a plate and let it cool completely.

3. Wipe the pan again and adjust the heat to medium-low. Place one tortilla in the pan. Using just half of the tortilla space, spread a quarter of the spinach, a quarter of the mushrooms, and a few slices of the mozzarella. When the filling is hot, the cheese is soft, and the bottom of the tortilla is speckled with golden spots, fold the tortilla in half and press it down with a flat spatula. Transfer to a plate. Repeat with the remaining ingredients. Slice the quesadillas into wedges and serve hot.

Ceviche with Tiger's Milk

One of the biggest contributions to world cuisine, ceviche originated in Peru, when native Indians realized that tossing fish with citrus juice helps preserve the fish and kills most bacteria. Fast forward a few centuries, ceviche is now one of the hottest dishes on menus across the world. I learned a cool trick from a Peruvian chef that I worked with, in which he actually ever so slightly blow torches the whole fish before cutting into small pieces. The reason for that is to release a dash of oil in the protein, making the fish a bit more tender.

When choosing the fish, be sure to smell it; it should smell fresh, almost salty like the ocean. And be sure it's clear of any dark spots, skin, and fat. It's important to let the fish "cook" in the lime juice without the vegetables, or, it will "cook" the vegetables as well, and they'll taste mushy.

The tiger's milk is the liquid that forms when the fish is cooking in lime juice. If you serve the ceviche with all of this liquid, then it becomes too watery. On the other hand, this liquid is full of flavor, so I like to add about a tablespoon or so back to the ceviche. I also like to add orange juice to the tiger's milk for extra flavor, and a dash of honey to balance out the tang of the citrus juice. **Serves 8**

1 pound super fresh white fleshed fish (such as halibut, sole, flounder, sea bass, red snapper)

6 tablespoons fresh lime juice

2 tablespoons orange juice

1/2 teaspoon honey

1 plum tomato, peeled, seeded, and finely diced

Half green bell pepper, finely chopped

1/3 cup red onion, finely chopped (about half an onion)

Kosher salt and freshly ground pepper

6 tablespoons fresh mint leaves, chopped

1/4 cup fresh cilantro, chopped

Extra-virgin olive oil for drizzling

1. When the fish is still whole, blow torch the fish so that it just starts to release oil, becoming slightly shinier, but still completely raw. The heat should be applied for all of 5 to 10 seconds. If you don't have a whole torch, hold the fish on top of a range flame on high, following the same concept.

2. Cut the fish into very small pieces, about 1/4-inch thick, and place in a bowl with the lime juice, orange juice, and honey. Make sure all pieces of fish are well covered and swimming in juices. Cover with a plastic wrap and chill for 20 minutes, not more than that.

3. In the meantime, place the tomato, bell pepper, and red onion in a bowl and season well with salt and pepper.

4. Using a colander or slotted spoon, remove the fish from the juice—now called Tiger's milk—reserving about 2 tablespoons of the liquid, and transfer fish to the bowl with vegetables. Add the herbs and about 1 tablespoon of the tiger's milk. Taste and adjust the seasoning with salt and pepper, maybe a bit more tiger's milk if you'd like.

5. Divide the ceviche among 8 small plates and drizzle a little bit of olive oil on top. Serve immediately.

Kale Gnocchi

Leticia Krause and I met over 20 years ago, when she was a student at CIA in upstate New York and I was a student at International Culinary Center (formerly French Culinary Institute). Two Leticias, two Brazilians, two friends sharing so many things in common and above all, our burning passion for cooking. Her family is originally from Italy and Germany, and they immigrated to the south of Brazil. She is living now in Bonito, a city located in Mato Grosso do Sul, where I went to visit her. Her cooking is an interesting mixture of Italian cooking with Brazilian ingredients. This kale gnocchi is inspired by one of the dishes she prepares with kale and Yucca. **Makes about 45 gnocchi**

2½ pounds fresh kale, stemmed

½ cup freshly grated Parmesan cheese (more for garnish)

½ cup yucca flour

2 eggs, lightly beaten

¼ cup all-purpose flour (more for coating)

Kosher salt and freshly ground pepper

Freshly ground nutmeg

Olive oil, for garnish

Micro lettuce or arugula, for garnish

1½ cups Tomato Sauce (page 165)

1. Bring a large pot of water to a boil and add a large pinch of salt. Add the kale and blanch until tender, about 4 minutes. Remove with a slotted spoon into a colander. Save about 1 ladle full of the hot cooking liquid. Run the kale under cold water to stop the cooking. Squeeze most of the water out. Transfer the kale to a food processor along with 2 to 3 tablespoons of the hot liquid and puree until smooth. You are looking for a green puree that is nice and smooth, but at this point it will not bind. You should have about 1 cup of green puree.

2. Using a rubber spatula, scrape the puree into a large bowl and add the Parmesan cheese, yucca flour, eggs, ¼ cup all-purpose flour, and season well with salt, pepper, and nutmeg. Work this dough really well; I like to use my hands for this task. I also like to test the seasoning, by cooking one dumpling in hot water before I continue mixing.

3. Dump the kale water and bring new water to a boil while you shape the dumplings.

4. Prepare two baking sheets: on one spread about 1 cup flour. Using a tablespoon, scoop the dumplings into little balls and make them oval, roll them in flour, and shake off the excess. Transfer to the other baking sheet. It's important to roll them in flour as it acts as a protection during cooking time, or the gnocchi could dissolve in the water.

5. Reduce the heat to low and bring water to a simmer. Add about half of the dumplings to the water and cook until they float up and are fully cooked, about 3 minutes. Using

a slotted spoon, transfer to a plate and cover with foil to keep moist. Repeat process with the remaining batch.

6. In another pan, heat the tomato sauce gently. At this point you can either drop the dumplings inside the tomato sauce and serve in a nice platter, or you can sauce some dinner plates and add the kale dumplings on top. Garnish with shaved Parmesan, a drizzle of olive oil, and some micro lettuce or herbs.

Watercress Flan

I ate many great dishes growing up in Rio de Janeiro. The great ones have seared themselves into my memory. I recall their scent, their flavors, and beauty, and revisit my astonishment at their perfection, even now, years later. I have a particular joyful memory of this watercress flan, which I ate over 20 years at C.T. (now called Olympe, the amazing restaurant from Chef Claude Troisgros), not only of what the dish tasted like, but how it made me feel. I was about 12 years old or so, it was one of the first times I was eating at a fancy restaurant, and I felt like I was graduating from kid's food to a chef's life. I dreamed of this flan, dream of it still, and it constantly inspires me to prepare interesting dishes with healthy ingredients.

There are three components to this recipe: the flan, the crepes, and the saffron sauce. You can prepare the flan and the crepes up to 5 days ahead of time, assemble completely, keep them wrapped in the refrigerator; bring to room temperature an hour before serving, and pop it in the oven for 5 to 7 minutes. I suggest you start by making the flan because according to the size of your flan mold, that is going to determine the size of crepe you need to make to be able to wrap it. **Serves 12**

For the Flan:
1 tablespoon olive oil
2 cloves garlic, minced
1 small shallot, minced
1 large bunch watercress (stems included), roughly chopped (save a few springs for garnish)
Kosher salt and freshly ground pepper
Freshly ground nutmeg
½ cup light sour cream
1 cup fat-free milk
½ cup heavy cream
4 whole eggs

For the Crepes:
1¼ cups fat-free milk
3 large eggs, lightly beaten
4 tablespoons unsalted butter, melted
1 cup whole wheat flour
Pinch of salt

Equipment: mini muffin pans to bake the flan, small omelet or crepe pan

Prepare the Flan:

1. In a large saucepan, warm the olive oil over low heat. Add the garlic and cook until it just starts to become golden, about 2 minutes. Add the shallot and cook until translucent, another 2 minutes. Add the watercress and mix everything with a wooden spoon, making sure the greens mix well with the onion mixture, about 1 minute (don't worry about cooking the watercress). Season with salt, pepper, and nutmeg.

2. Pour in the sour cream, milk, and heavy cream, bring to a quick boil, and then turn the heat off. Cover the pan and set aside. Let it steep for 15 minutes. Taste the liquid before blending and adjust the seasoning as needed.

3. Working in batches, puree the watercress mixture in a blender. When the whole mixture is pureed, slowly pour it directly into a strainer set over a large measuring cup. Push the liquid through the strainer. You should have about 2 cups. If you have a little extra liquid, discard; if you have a little less than 2 cups, complete with fat-free milk. Let the liquid cool to room temperature before adding the eggs.

For the Saffron Butter Sauce:

6 tablespoons water

½ stick unsalted butter, cold, cut into cubes

½ teaspoon saffron threads

4. Preheat the oven to 225°F on the convection mode. If you don't have convection in your oven, prepare a water bath and raise the temperature to 325°F.

5. Pour the strained watercress and eggs in the blender and pulse until well mixed. Season one more time with salt and pepper. Carefully pour into the mini muffin-pan and bake for 25 to 35 minutes, until set. Let it cool at room temperature, then chill. The flan can be prepared up to 5 days ahead of time and kept wrapped in plastic film in the refrigerator.

(Continued on next page)

Prepare the Crepes:

1. In a bowl, mix together milk, eggs, and melted butter.

2. In a separate bowl, place the flour and a pinch of salt, make a well in the center, and pour in the wet mixture. Whisk well until smooth.

3. Pass through a fine sieve strainer, pressing down with a rubber spatula.

4. Chill for 30 minutes.

5. On very low heat, place an omelet pan and pour 2 tablespoons of crepe batter. Swirl the pan in a circular movement, making sure the crepe is nice and round, thin and evenly spread. Let it cook just until is set. Do not let the crepe get any color. Turn the crepe on the other side— you might be able to use your hands, since the heat is so low, and again, cook the crepe just until is set.

6. Repeat the process. This batter will make around 14 to 16 crepes.

7. **Assemble the Wrap:** Place each flan inside a crepe and bring the edges of the crepe to the center, pressing gently. Turn it upside down so that the seam is facing down. Repeat the process. This step can be done up to 3 days ahead of time and kept in a plastic container covered with a tight lid.

Make the Saffron Sauce:

1. In a medium sized saucepan, over low heat, warm water. Add butter pieces and whisk well, making sure the sauce does not boil at any point, so the sauce doesn't break. Add the saffron and whisk well. Season with salt and pepper.

2. To serve, heat the crepe in a preheated oven for 5 to 7 minutes, place a small amount of sauce around, and garnish with a watercress leaf on top.

Salads and Soups

Bok Choy Salad with Sunflower Seeds   81

Shitake Carpaccio   83

Chayote Salad with Quinoa and Mustard Vinaigrette   84

Hearts of Palm and Spinach Salad   85

Grilled Eggplant with Minas Cheese and Cilantro   87

Wheatberry Waldorf Salad   89

Spinach Soup with Egg Salad   90

Orange Salad with Pumpkin Seeds and Crumbled *Queso-Blanco*   93

Sweet Potato and Green Bean Salad   95

Hearty Black Bean Soup   97

Sopa Seca   99

Kale Gorgonzola Salad   100

Chicken Tortilla Soup   101

Celery Salad   105

Watermelon Carpaccio with Feta Cheese, Olives, Cilantro, and Arugula   107

Addictive *Cucumba* Salad   109

Bok Choy Salad with Sunflower Seeds

My neighbor Randi Regenstein is a social butterfly who loves to party. I often tell her she should have been born in Brazil, for she is always ready for a celebration. At a recent BBQ, she prepared this delicious salad, and I couldn't get over how different it is. When I asked for the recipe, she told me that the secret here is to dress and toss the salad at least 20 minutes before serving, so that all flavors can mingle, and the rice and vegetables have a chance to soften. **Serves 4**

For the Salad:

1 cup wild rice

1 large bok choy

3 scallions, green and white parts, chopped finely

³/₄ cup sunflower seeds

³/₄ cup sliced almonds

Kosher salt and freshly ground black pepper

For the Dressing:

3 tablespoons soy sauce

¹/₃ cup white wine vinegar

¹/₄ cup turbinado sugar

³/₄ cup olive oil

1. **Cook the Wild Rice:** Place it in a medium pan and cover with water, at least 2 inches above the rice level. Cover the pan, bring to a boil, then reduce to low and simmer until the rice is tender, about 45 minutes. Drain and set aside to let it cool.

2. Cut the bok choy into ³/₄-inch pieces and place in a bowl; add the scallions, sunflower seeds, almonds, and cooled wild rice.

3. Combine the soy sauce, white wine vinegar, and coconut sugar in a blender. With the machine on, add the oil in a slow steady stream until it comes together. Transfer to a container until ready to use. This sauce can be done up to 5 days ahead of time.

4. Pour just enough dressing over the salad mixture and toss to combine. Taste and season lightly with salt and pepper. Let the salad sit for at least 20 minutes before serving. Serve slightly chilled or at room temperature.

Shitake Carpaccio

Although the classic carpaccio is made with beef (the recipe originated in Venice back in the 1950s in honor of an Italian painter called Vittore Carpaccio), in this day and age, you can find carpaccio of anything. Just slice food paper thin, top it with olive oil, lemon, Parmesan, and herbs, and you have a carpaccio. Even fruit gets in the mix (and I love them!).

This recipe is inspired by Thomas Troisgros in Rio de Janeiro. When washing mushrooms, don't let them sit under the water as they tend to absorb it. Rinse as fast as you can, and air-dry them. **Serves 4**

2 slices whole wheat bread, crusts removed and cut into $\frac{1}{4}$-inch cubes

6 tablespoons olive oil

Kosher salt and freshly ground black pepper

$\frac{3}{4}$ pound shitake mushrooms, stems removed, rinsed briefly and dried

1 small clove garlic

$\frac{1}{2}$ teaspoon soy sauce

1 tablespoon lime juice (about 1 lime)

4 tablespoons freshly grated Parmesan cheese

3 tablespoons freshly chopped parsley

1 tablespoon black sesame seeds

1. Preheat the oven to 350°F. Place the bread cubes on a baking sheet and drizzle 2 tablespoons of olive oil on top. Season with salt and pepper and toss. Toast in the oven until it just begins to get crunchy, about 15 minutes, mixing once during baking time.

2. Slice the mushrooms as thin as possible with a chef's knife or mandoline and arrange the slices onto 4 serving plates. Season lightly with salt and pepper.

3. With the back of a knife, smash the garlic with a pinch of salt into a paste. Combine the garlic paste, soy sauce, and lime juice in a small bowl. Whisk in the remaining 4 tablespoons of olive oil to form an emulsion. Drizzle the vinaigrette over the mushroom slices.

4. Top with Parmesan cheese, croutons, parsley, and sesame seeds. Let sit for 5 to 10 minutes before serving for the flavors to mingle. Serve at room temperature.

Chayote Salad with Quinoa and Mustard Vinaigrette

Chayote is beginning to appear more often in stores and it's worth giving it a try because it's so delicious! The chayote gets crunchy as it loses its water in the de-salting process, and the mustard vinaigrette enrobes every bit of vegetable in a silky and rich way. **Serves 4**

1 cup uncooked red quinoa
3 medium chayote (about 8½ ounces each) peeled and julienned
Kosher salt
2 tablespoons lime juice (about 1 lime)
1 teaspoon Dijon mustard
1 tablespoon light sour cream
⅓ cup extra-virgin olive oil
Freshly ground black pepper
½ cup pomegranate kernels
¼ cup freshly chopped chives or dill

1. Cook quinoa according to package directions. Drain and place in a large bowl. Let it cool for 30 minutes.

2. Place the chayote in a medium colander sitting inside a bowl, sprinkle with kosher salt, and toss. Let sit and drain for at least 30 minutes.

3. Meanwhile, prepare the vinaigrette: place the lime juice, mustard, and sour cream in a medium bowl. Gradually whisk in the oil to create an emulsion. Season with salt and pepper. This vinaigrette can be prepared up to 3 days ahead of time and stored in a plastic container covered with a tight-fitting lid in the refrigerator.

4. In a bowl, mix the drained chayote and cooled quinoa. Pour enough vinaigrette over, add the pomegranate and chives, and toss well. Serve slightly chilled or at room temperature.

Hearts of Palm and Spinach Salad

It wasn't that long ago that healthy meant boring foods of questionable portion or something packed with a big hemp leaf on it. Who would have guessed that now, we'd be savoring salads as healthy as they are delicious. Consider this salad of spinach and hearts of palm. It comes together so fast! You can find canned hearts of palm easily these days in any regular supermarket. However, if you have the chance to source fresh hearts of palm (try Melissa's Produce) then all of a sudden, this salad goes to a whole different level. **Serves 4**

For the Vinaigrette:
1 tablespoon white wine
   vinegar (or rice vinegar)
2 teaspoons lime juice
1 tablespoon soy sauce
$\frac{1}{2}$ teaspoon Dijon mustard
$\frac{1}{2}$ teaspoon sugar
3 tablespoons sunflower oil
1 tablespoon sesame oil
Kosher salt and freshly ground
   black pepper

For the Salad:
2 (14-ounce) cans hearts of
   palm (about $\frac{1}{2}$ pound),
   drained and cut into
   $\frac{1}{2}$-inch rounds
12 ounces fresh spinach
1 tablespoon sesame seeds,
   lightly toasted

1. In a bowl, whisk together the vinegar, lime juice, soy sauce, mustard, and sugar. Gradually whisk in the oils, a little at a time, until the sauce is creamy and blended. Season lightly with salt and pepper. This vinaigrette can be prepared up to 3 days ahead of time and stored in a plastic container covered with a tight-fitting lid in the refrigerator.

2. Just before serving, place the spinach and hearts of palm in a large bowl and pour just enough dressing around the bowl. Toss to coat evenly. Be careful not to over dress, or the salad will turn mushy quite fast. Plate and sprinkle with sesame seeds on each plate.

Grilled Eggplant with Minas Cheese and Cilantro

If we're in Latin land, and eggplant is the main ingredient, then I'm in safe territory adding crumbling queso-blanco and cilantro. The eggplant absorbs plenty of oil on the grill and becomes irresistible. I use globe eggplant for this recipe, but feel free to make good use of your trips to the farmer's market and choose any other variety of eggplant. You can grill the eggplant ahead of time and assemble the salad just before serving. **Serves 4 to 6**

1 large globe eggplant (about 1 lb), ends removed, and sliced into ½-inch thick rounds

6 tablespoons extra-virgin olive oil

Kosher salt and freshly ground black pepper

1 scallion, white and green parts, finally chopped

1½ tablespoons fresh lime juice (about 1 lime)

¼ cup crumbled *queso-blanco* (or feta cheese)

4 tablespoons freshly chopped cilantro

1. Heat your grill to high and oil with cooking spray.

2. Brush both sides of the eggplant slices with 3 tablespoons of the olive oil and season each with salt and pepper.

3. Grill the eggplant, until lightly charred, about 3 minutes per side. Transfer to a platter.

4. Place the scallion and lime juice in a medium bowl. Whisk in the remaining 3 tablespoons olive oil and season lightly with salt and pepper. Drizzle on top of the eggplants.

5. Top with the cheese and garnish with cilantro. Serve at room temperature.

Wheatberry Waldorf Salad

There was a time when you'd think of salad and you'd think of a bowl of greens. Celeiro, a restaurant in Rio de Janeiro, started making grain salads back in the '80s, when it opened. It was way ahead of its time and has been in the same location for over 40 years. I recall many times when I was forced to have my meal standing almost shoulder to shoulder with other patrons, because the limited space gets so unbearably crowded. And I keep asking myself, why should I ever consider going back to such an uncomfortable place? The truth is that I do, and the more I do, the more I love it. Why? The food is just amazing. In my opinion, grain salads are more of a concept than a dish. Celeiro is proof. There are infinite variations. Cook some grains (in this case, wheatberries), throw any chopped vegetables, fruits, nuts, cheese, and call it a grain salad. This recipe features classic flavors: apple, celery, scallions, and nuts. The rest is trivial: parsley, and a lovely mustard vinaigrette. You can't go wrong! **Serves 8**

For the Vinaigrette:
4 tablespoons white wine vinegar
4 teaspoons Dijon mustard
½ teaspoon mustard seeds
1 teaspoon honey
Kosher salt and freshly ground
    pepper
¾ cup extra-virgin olive oil

For the Salad:
1 cup raw wheatberries
2 cups cubed apple
    (about 1 large apple)
1 cup diced celery
    (about 4 stalks)
1 scallion, white and green parts,
    finely chopped
½ cup fresh chopped parsley
1 cup pecans, lightly toasted and
    roughly chopped

1. **Prepare the Vinaigrette:** In a small bowl, whisk together the vinegar, mustard, seeds, and honey. Season with salt and pepper. Slowly whisk in the oil, in a steady stream, until the sauce is creamy and blended. Taste and adjust the flavor.

2. Place the wheatberries in a medium pan and cover with water, at least 2 inches above the grain level. Cover the pan, bring to a boil, then reduce heat to low and simmer until the wheatberries are tender, about 45 minutes. Drain, set aside, and cool completely.

3. In a large bowl, mix the cooled wheatberries with the apple, celery, scallion, and parsley. Add enough vinaigrette to cover and moisten every grain of wheatberry and taste to adjust the seasoning. Add more salt and pepper if necessary. Add the pecans and serve slightly cold or at room temperature.

Spinach Soup with Egg Salad

The combination of spinach and egg happens in so many ways that I thought, why not bring it to a healthy and delicious soup? And the result is fantastic! You can use fresh spinach or frozen. If you use frozen, make sure to thaw it before and squeeze all the water out. If you use fresh spinach, make sure you wash it and dry it really well. You can use a salad spinner or just rinse then spread the leaves on a tray to dry out for 10 minutes. It's also important to remove the stems if they are too big, as they can be chewy to eat. **Serves 4**

2 cups reduced-sodium chicken stock (store-bought or homemade)
1 cup fat-free milk
4 tablespoons olive oil
4 cloves garlic, finely minced
1 medium onion, roughly chopped
¼ pound red potatoes, peeled and quartered
5 ounces spinach leaves
Kosher salt and freshly ground pepper
Freshly grated nutmeg
2 hard-boiled eggs
1 teaspoon finely chopped shallot
1 stalk celery, finely chopped
Parsley leaves for garnish
4 teaspoons sour cream, for garnish

1. In a medium pan, combine the chicken stock and milk, cover the pan, and bring to a simmer for 5 minutes.

2. In another large pan, warm 3 tablespoons of the olive oil on low heat and add the garlic. Cook, stirring frequently with a wooden spoon, until it just starts to get golden.

3. Add the onion and continue cooking, stirring, until it's soft and translucent, about 5 minutes.

4. Add the potatoes, turn the heat just a dash higher (but not high), and cook until the potatoes are hot, about 4 minutes.

5. Pour the liquid over the vegetables, cover, and cook on a gentle heat until potatoes are completely tender, about 10 minutes.

6. Bring the soup to a boil, add the spinach, and let it cook for 2 minutes.

7. Working in batches, pour ladles of soup into a blender and puree the mixture until completely smooth. Season to taste with salt and pepper, and nutmeg.

8. While the soup is simmering, prepare the topping: chop the hard-boiled eggs, and combine in a bowl with shallot, celery, and parsley. Drizzle with the remaining 1 tablespoon olive oil.

9. Serve the soup in bowls and top with egg salad, parsley leaves, a dollop of sour cream, and some freshly ground pepper.

Orange Salad with Pumpkin Seeds and Crumbled Queso-Blanco

Hello yellow! Don't be fooled by the simplicity of oranges. If you are willing to take superfoods to the next level, start looking at oranges with a different perspective, because beauty lives in raw food. This salad is a tribute to one of the most common staples of produce in any grocery store, and is a breeze to make. Dazzle with a lovely vinaigrette, sprinkle with pumpkin seeds and queso-blanco, and you have just punched the ticket to a healthy lifestyle! **Serves 4**

For the Dressing:

3 tablespoons freshly
   squeezed orange juice
1 tablespoon white wine
   vinegar
1 tablespoon honey
1 teaspoon orange zest
1 teaspoon finely minced
   shallots
Kosher salt and freshly ground
   black pepper
2 tablespoons olive oil

For the Salad:

3 navel oranges
¼ cup roasted pumpkin seeds
¼ cup crumbled *queso-blanco*
   (or feta cheese or goat
   cheese)
2 tablespoons freshly
   chopped cilantro leaves
1 teaspoon hemp seeds

1. Whisk together the orange juice, vinegar, honey, orange zest, shallots, and season with salt and pepper. Drizzle in the olive oil in a steady stream to create an emulsion. Set aside.

2. Using a serrated knife, cut away a thin slice from top and bottom of the oranges. Stand the orange up and work your knife around the contour of the fruit, cutting away the peel without removing too much of the flesh. Once peeled, cut them into rounds, about ⅓- to ½-inch thick, and arrange them attractively on a platter.

3. Drizzle with the dressing, sprinkle the pumpkin seeds, *queso-blanco*, cilantro, and hemp seeds. Serve immediately.

Sweet Potato and Green Bean Salad

What a beautiful mix of colors, textures, and flavors you'll find in this Ecuadorian-inspired sweet potato salad. It's quite easy to make when you plan ahead. Make this recipe on a Sunday for week day lunches and you're set for the week! **Serves 4**

2 sweet potatoes, peeled and cubed

2 tablespoons + ¼ cup extra-virgin olive oil

Kosher salt and freshly ground pepper

¼ pound string beans, both ends trimmed

2 scallions, sliced thinly on a bias

1 shallot, minced

½ small red onion, thinly sliced

½ garlic, finely mined

1 cup cooked black beans

2 tablespoons fresh lemon juice

1 tablespoon Dijon mustard

¼ cup chopped fresh parsley

2 tablespoons sunflower seeds

1. Prepare the sweet potatoes: Preheat the oven to 400°F. Put the cubed potatoes on a large baking sheet; drizzle with 2 tablespoons olive oil, ensuring all of the cubes are coated. Spread the potatoes in a single layer. Roast for 25 to 30 minutes, until the potatoes are tender and browned, stirring them halfway. Set aside.

2. Blanch the green beans: Bring a large pot of water to a boil, add a large pinch of salt, and add the string beans. Cook on medium heat until just tender, about 3 minutes. Transfer to a bowl of iced water. Set aside for 5 minutes. Remove from the ice water and spread the beans on a plate covered with paper towels to absorb any extra water. Let it air dry for 5 minutes, then chop it roughly. You should have about 1 cup.

3. In a large bowl, stir together the scallions, shallot, red onion, and garlic. Stir the potatoes, green beans, and black beans into the onion mixture and set aside.

4. In a small bowl, whisk together the remaining ¼ cup olive oil, lemon juice, and mustard. Drizzle the vinaigrette over the salad and toss gently. Season with salt and pepper. Stir in the parsley, sprinkle with sunflower seeds, and serve immediately.

Hearty Black Bean Soup

As a good Latin woman, I keep lots of bean bags in my pantry. Though I've written this recipe, I'll be the first to tell you that you don't need a recipe to make this soup. Mark this page with a sticky note and work your way through it. Use it the first time, maybe the second, but after that, you can remove that sticky note—you'll never need a recipe for bean soup again. Promise.

And you need no special equipment, ingredients, or really much time either. I love black beans, but you can use just about any beans you have on hand. You want to cook this recipe long enough to develop the flavors, but not that long that it will lose its freshness. This type of soup is super healthy and tastes great, and even better the next day. It also freezes very well, so by all means, consider making a double batch for those days when you don't want to cook. **Serves 4**

3 tablespoons extra-virgin olive oil

3 cloves garlic, finely minced garlic

1 onion, finely chopped onion

$\frac{1}{2}$ cup finely chopped celery

1 cup finely chopped carrots

Kosher salt and fresh black pepper

$\frac{1}{2}$ teaspoon freshly grated nutmeg

$\frac{1}{2}$ teaspoon cumin

4 cups chicken or vegetable stock

4 cups cooked black beans

2 tablespoons fresh chopped parsley

1. In a large soup pot, warm the olive oil over low heat and add the garlic. Cook, stirring constantly, until it's just golden brown, about 2 minutes.

2. Add the onion, celery, and carrots, and cook, stirring frequently, until the vegetables are soft and translucent, about 5 minutes. Season lightly with salt, pepper, nutmeg, and cumin, and continue cooking.

3. Add the stock, cover, and bring to a boil over high heat.

4. Reduce the heat to low and add the beans. Cover the soup and simmer for 30 to 45 minutes, checking seasoning and liquid level. If you need more liquid, add water or more chicken stock.

5. Sprinkle with fresh parsley and serve hot.

Sopa Seca

This dish is not exactly a soup, not exactly a pasta dish, but something in between. Like the name says, it's a "dry" soup, or a soup that carries less liquid than usual, though you can always add a few more tablespoons water as the pasta and beans absorb all the liquid. Make sure to use good quality spinach, even if it's frozen (and thawed), because it really adds an important touch to the recipe. When it comes to cheese, I like to finish with a combination of Parmesan and queso-blanco, but feel free to use whatever combination you prefer. As for the pasta, traditionally this dish is made with fideos, but I like a short pasta better, like shells; feel free any shape you choose. **Serves 6 to 8**

2 tablespoons olive oil
2 cloves garlic, minced finely
1/2 red onion, chopped fine
1 small shallot, chopped finely
3 scallions, chopped finely
1/2 teaspoon Spanish paprika
1 teaspoon dried oregano
1/2 teaspoon ground cumin
3 plum tomatoes, peeled, seeded, and roughly chopped
Kosher salt
Freshly ground pepper
1 (15-ounce) can chickpeas
8 ounces pasta (3 1/2 cups medium shells)
3 cups low sodium chicken or vegetable broth
1 pound spinach, steamed and chopped coarsely (or frozen, thawed, chopped)
1/2 cup Parmesan cheese
1/2 cup *queso-blanco* (or feta cheese), crumbled
3 tablespoons fresh chopped parsley

1. In a large pot, add 2 tablespoons of the olive oil on low heat and cook the garlic gently over low heat until it just starts to turn golden, about 2 minutes.

2. Add the red onion, shallot, scallions, paprika, oregano, and cumin, and cook everything, stirring with a wooden spoon, until the flavors meld together.

3. Add the chopped tomatoes and cook for another 3 minutes.

4. Season lightly with salt and pepper

5. Add the chickpeas and pasta (yes, uncooked), and cook with the vegetable mixture until they meet each other's flavors and get hot, about 5 minutes.

6. Pour in the broth and cover the pan, cooking at a gentle simmer, checking and stirring often, until the pasta is tender, about 10 to 12 minutes.

7. Add the spinach, a handful at a time, and continue to cook, stirring occasionally, until flavors are well distributed and fragrant.

8. Just before serving, remove from the heat and sprinkle both cheeses all over and cover the soup, allowing the cheese to melt, about 3 to 5 minutes.

9. Garnish with parsley before serving.

Kale Gorgonzola Salad

High above Rio's famed beaches, in the mountain's fertile quiet heartland, the hills are piney, the air is scented with eucalyptus, and home cooks still depend solely on the farmer's market to get fresh ingredients. The first thing to notice at the retreat town of Teresópolis is the silence. The second is the cooking. The greens in this region are incredible. This recipe comes from Patricia Gonzales, a home cook from Teresópolis. I have tasted this recipe at least 3 times, and each time, she uses a different kind of greens. I invite you to do the same. Make it with spinach, kale, arugula, or frisee. Or combine different lettuces. Whatever greens you have on hand, this salad is simple and amazing; mashing the cheese in the olive oil creates a creamy dressing that's absolutely delicious! **Serves 4**

¼ cup crumbled gorgonzola
5 tablespoons + 1 teaspoon
  extra-virgin olive oil
2 twists fresh black pepper
5 cups kale leaves
⅓ cup chopped almonds

1. Place the gorgonzola in a bowl and pour the olive oil on top along with the fresh pepper. Using a fork or any other mashing tool, mash together until it becomes a paste.

2. Add the kale and now using tongs, toss everything together. Let it stand for 5 minutes.

3. Arrange kale leaves on a plate or platter. Top with almonds and serve.

Chicken Tortilla Soup

When I was in Los Cabos, Mexico, I ate a tortilla soup that was absolutely delicious, mildly spicy, and with a deep tomato flavor. The chicken breast is shredded thinly and becomes very silky swimming in the tomato soup. While you can make the soup with canned crushed tomatoes, I'd much rather use fresh tomatoes. I like using just a little bit of chipotle chile in adobo sauce; this way my kids enjoy as well (they'll eat spicy foods but in moderation). If you like your tortilla soup hotter than mine, feel free to use more than 2 chipotle chiles, or even a whole can. If you don't care to hunt for it, just substitute 2 tablespoons chipotle chile powder.

I usually keep this soup on the simple side, using chicken, queso-blanco, cilantro, and tortilla as garnishes, but you can be creative and go crazy with all of the extra stuff you can put in the soup: avocados, sour cream, or more cheese. You can serve the side dishes in small bowls and people can add whatever they want to the soup. It's a fun dish to eat! **Serves 4 to 6**

For the Soup:
2 tablespoons olive oil
2 cloves garlic, minced
2 yellow onions, peeled and
    roughly chopped
Kosher salt and freshly ground
    pepper
Freshly ground nutmeg
1$\frac{1}{2}$ pounds plum tomatoes (or
    a 28-ounce can crushed
    tomatoes), roughly chopped
2 chipotle chiles in adobo
    sauce, seeded and coarsely
    chopped
8 cups chicken stock
2 cooked chicken breasts
    shredded, about 2$\frac{1}{2}$–3 cups

For the Tortillas:
6 wheat-flour tortillas, cut into
    thin strips (about $\frac{1}{2}$-inch)
$\frac{1}{4}$ cup canola oil for frying

For the Garnish:
$\frac{1}{4}$ cup freshly chopped cilantro
8 ounces queso fresco
    (or feta cheese)

1. **Prepare the Soup:** In a large saucepan, pour the olive oil over medium heat and cook the garlic until just lightly golden brown, about 2 minutes.

2. Add the onions and mix, stirring occasionally with a wooden spoon, and cook until soft and translucent, about 4 minutes. Season with salt, pepper, and nutmeg.

3. Add the tomatoes and cook, until they start to soften and mush down.

4. Add the chopped chipotles and mix well.

5. Pour the chicken stock and simmer the soup, covered, over low heat, checking occasionally, until the tomatoes are very soft, about 30 minutes.

6. In the meantime, fry the tortillas: In a nonstick skillet, warm the oil over medium heat. Add the tortilla strips in batches, stirring, until golden and crisp. Be careful that the tortillas don't get too dark, or else they burn. Using tongs or a slotted spoon, transfer the tortillas to a plate lined with parchment paper. I like to sprinkle a little salt as they come out of the pan. Repeat the process until all tortillas are golden.

7. Check the soup and turn off the heat. Working in batches, puree the soup in a blender, until it's nice and smooth. If soup is way too hot for the blender, let the soup breathe for 5 minutes before pureeing.

(Continued on page 103)

8. At this point, you can either return the soup to the pan, or you can strain it to make sure is a bit silkier.

9. Pour the pureed soup back in the pot and simmer gently.

10. Add the shredded chicken and simmer until chicken is soft and tender, about 5 minutes.

11. Taste and adjust the seasoning. Ladle the soup into individual bowls and garnish with *queso-blanco*, cilantro, and tortillas.

Celery Salad

This first time I tasted Ignacio Matto's cooking, I wasn't sure where he was from. The talented chef is from Uruguay and runs the amazing kitchen of Estela, one of my favorite restaurants in New York City. After eating there, I learned a few lessons: first, that it's foolish to think that every Latin chef cooks recipes that scream Latin flavors—Latin can be a subtle thing. Second, that some dishes simply have the ability to knock down the barriers between you and happiness. And third, that our brains can actually crave for certain salads. One dish that epitomizes the cravings for a healthy salad is this crispy celery salad, inspired by Ignacio Matto's recipe.

Feel free to use any cheese of your preference; I used Pecorino Velathri, which is a softer Pecorino, but I've made this salad with a variety of cheeses: queso-blanco, feta cheese, Pecorino Romano, Parmesan, blue cheese, and Gorgonzola. The amount of cheese is small; it's here just to add a kick. I like to cut the celery thin, but honestly, that doesn't even matter much because the flavor of the celery shines at any reasonable thickness. Salad your way to happiness! **Serves 4**

2 bunches celery with leaves
Kosher salt and freshly ground
   black pepper
2 tablespoons fresh lemon
   juice
1 tablespoon Dijon mustard
1/4 cup extra-virgin olive oil,
   plus more to drizzle
1/4 cup fresh mint leaves,
   roughly chopped
4 teaspoons hemp seeds
4 ounces Pecorino Velathri

1. Cut the bottom off the celery bunch and discard. Pick the leaves of the celery: the greener the better, but it's nice to use some of the inner, more yellow leaves as well, to give a nice mixture. Chop the leaves roughly and reserve them in the fridge until ready to assemble the salad. Separate the stalks and rinse them in cold water. Using a vegetable peeler, peel each stalk, removing the outer fiber. Cut the celery into thin slices on a bias and place them in a colander with a plate underneath. Sprinkle kosher salt all over, toss, and let it rest in the fridge for 20 minutes to crisp up and open the celery for dressing.

2. In the meantime, prepare the vinaigrette: place the lemon juice and mustard in a bowl with salt and pepper. Slowly pour the olive oil, whisking all the while to create an emulsion.

3. Transfer celery to a bowl, add enough vinaigrette to coat really well and enrobe every piece of celery. Add the chopped mint and celery leaves.

4. Distribute the celery among the plates and spread them out to cover the entire surface of the plate. Drizzle some more vinaigrette on top, and a few drops of olive oil.

5. Scatter the hemp seeds and Pecorino. You want to enough cheese to cover the salad, but not overwhelm it. Finish with black pepper.

Watermelon Carpaccio with Feta Cheese, Olives, Cilantro, and Arugula

Dinner course meets dinner rush: because we are well-versed in the kitchen and not afraid to throw something together in a jiff, and still call it a delicious meal. Like this newly imagined salad. There is a new trend in Latin America; we're turning everything into a carpaccio. In this book, for example, you will find Shitake Carpaccio (page 83); the Celery Salad (page 105) I think of as a carpaccio as well, even the Orange Salad with Pumpkin Seeds and Crumbled Queso-Blanco on page 93, is a type of carpaccio. Slice it thin, make it beautiful, make it healthy, and call it a carpaccio! **Serves 4**

For the Dressing:

2 tablespoons olive oil
3 tablespoons Kalamata olives, pitted and finely chopped
1 teaspoon minced shallots (about ½ shallot)
2 tablespoons freshly chopped cilantro leaves
Kosher salt and freshly ground black pepper

For the Salad:

1 pound watermelon in one big chunk
¼ cup crumbled *queso-blanco* (or feta cheese)
1 teaspoon hemp seeds
2 cups arugula

1. Whisk together the olives, shallots, and cilantro. Season with salt and pepper. Drizzle in the olive oil in a steady stream to create an emulsion. Set aside.

2. Using a long knife, cut away thin slices of watermelon. Try to cut them as long as you can, and feel free to overlap them on the plate.

3. Drizzle with the dressing; sprinkle cheese and hemp seeds. Top with arugula and serve immediately.

Addictive Cucumba Salad

I love languages! In my opinion, language is a huge part of a culture, just like music and cooking. I share this love of languages with a friend, Sheldon Kirsh, who speaks seven languages fluently!

Recently, he introduced me to a restaurant in New York City that represents a beautiful blend of cooking and languages. Sen Sakana is a Peruvian-Japanese blend of cuisines; on the plate, through the décor, and in the faces of the people. My conversation with Sheldon is all over the place—it's a mixture of English and Portuguese with a few words in Hebrew, a few words in French, and lots of words in Spanish. When we ordered this addictive cucumber salad over lunch, we couldn't stop raving about it: it's delicioso! C'est maginifique! Riquisimo! Que espetaculo! I'm addicted! Vou tentar fazer na minha cozinha! And so, I did try to make it at home, inspired by our multi-language lunch, and let me tell you something: the only word you really need to say here is cucumba! Now let's get cooking and you'll see how easy this is. **Serves 4**

2 English cucumbers
Kosher salt
2 tablespoons cooked quinoa
2 tablespoons freshly squeezed lime juice (about 2 limes)
1 tablespoon *aji amarilo* paste (I used Peru Food)
¼ cup extra-virgin olive oil
Freshly ground black pepper
2 tablespoons mixed sesame seeds
¼ teaspoon paprika, for garnish
4 tablespoons microgreens, for garnish, optional

A note about the aji paste: Using just a teaspoon of this typical Latin food gives a wonderful kick without overwhelming the salad.

1. Cut off the ends and peel the cucumbers. Slice it into ¼-inch thick slices and place in a colander over a plate. Sprinkle with kosher salt, toss well, and let it sit for about 20 minutes, until water drains and cucumber becomes crunchy.

2. In the meantime, on a nonstick skillet, toast the quinoa over medium heat, mixing occasionally, until it becomes slightly crunchy, about 5 minutes. Be careful not to burn the quinoa.

3. Place the lime juice and aji paste in a bowl. Pour the olive oil in a steady stream and whisk constantly to create an emulsion. Season lightly with salt and pepper.

4. Try the cucumber and make sure it's crunchy. Arrange a row of cucumbers on each plate. I like to use rectangular plates for this recipe; if you use round plates, arrange the cucumber slices in a circle to look pretty. Drizzle the vinaigrette on top and around the plate. Sprinkle the sesame seeds, toasted quinoa, and dust with paprika all over. Garnish with microgreens or any other herb you might have handy. Serve immediately. And cheer in whatever language you'd like!

Chicken Tamale Pie, page 119

Poultry

Arroz con Pollo   112

Ropa Vieja de Pollo   115

Warm Cucumber Chicken Salad   117

Turkey Sausage with Bell Peppers   118

Chicken Tamale Pie   119

Chicken in a Pot   123

Chicken Barley Stew   124

Chicken, Cashew, and Red Pepper Stir Fry   126

Chicken with Peas and Potatoes   127

Turkey with Mole Sauce   129

Coffee-Rubbed Chicken Breast with Corn Salsa   133

Grilled Chicken Drumstick with Orange Glaze   135

Chicken Stew with Tomatillos and Cilantro   137

Picadillo de Pollo   139

Roasted Chicken Breast with Guava BBQ Sauce   140

Braised Chicken with Fennel and Oranges   142

Quinoa with Chicken Sausage and Mushrooms   144

Papas y Salsicha Criollo   147

Arroz con Pollo

If I had to choose one recipe from the classic Latin repertoire to serve as an example of all the substitutions that can be made to health-ify a recipe, this is it. Arroz con Pollo is an incredible delicious dish, full of flavor, and full of satisfaction. The original recipe is not all that fatty, but depending on the type of sausage, chicken, and rice you eat, it might be on the edge for those concerned with losing weight or type 2 diabetes.

By using brown rice, chicken or turkey sausage, and skinless-less chicken breasts, it becomes a lot more diabetes-friendly recipe. At the same time, you don't sacrifice flavor, as the herbs and spices are here in full gear. **Serves 6 to 8**

For the Chicken:
3 large cloves garlic
2 teaspoons kosher salt
2 tablespoons lime juice
2 teaspoons dried oregano
4 skinless chicken breasts

For the Rice:
Freshly ground black pepper
3 tablespoons olive oil
3 ounces turkey or chicken
    sausage, cut into 1/4-inch-
    thick slices
2 medium onions, diced
3 scallions, green and white
    parts, chopped
3 large cloves garlic, minced
1 teaspoon paprika
2 bay leaves
4–5 plum tomatoes, peeled,
    seeded, and chopped finely
2 cups brown rice such as
    jasmine
2 1/2 cups reduced-sodium
    chicken broth
1/4 cup fresh chopped parsley

Prepare the Chicken Marinade:
1. Mince and mash garlic into a paste with 2 teaspoons salt, then transfer to a large bowl. Stir in lime juice and oregano. Add the chicken pieces and rub all over with marinade, until well coated. Cover with plastic wrap and leave at room temperature for 1 to 2 hours.

Cook the Chicken and Rice:
1. Spread chicken over a sheet pan covered with paper towels and pat dry. Season with freshly ground pepper on both sides.

2. In a large heavy pot (at least 12 inches wide) over medium heat, warm 2 tablespoons of the olive oil. Cook the chicken skin side down until lightly browned all over, about 3 minutes per side.

3. Using a slotted spoon, transfer chicken to a bowl and cover with foil to keep moist.

4. If there is too much fat, drain a little. If there are too many pieces of garlic stuck to the pan, deglaze with a little water, about 1/2 cup, scraping the bottom of the pan and bring to boil.

5. Warm the remaining 1 tablespoon of olive oil over medium heat and cook the sausage until lightly brown on both sides, about 2 minutes per side. Use the same slotted spoon to transfer the sausage to the bowl with the chicken. Cover again.

6. Reduce the heat to low and add the onions and scallions. Cook until soft and tender, mixing occasionally with a wooden spoon and scraping the bottom of the pan, about 2 minutes. Add the garlic and cook for another minute.

7. Add the paprika, bay leaves, and tomatoes, and cook everything together until soft and tender, about 4 to 5 minutes.

8. Add the rice and stir well, making sure every grain is shiny and well mixed into the vegetable mixture. If you would like to use the deglazing juices from the chicken, now is the time.

9. Add the broth and bring to a boil. Reduce the heat to low, add the chicken pieces, sausage, and any juice that accumulated in the bowl, arranging evenly all over the rice. Season with salt and pepper, cover, and cook gently until rice has absorbed all the liquid, about 20 to 30 minutes.

10. Garnish with parsley.

Ropa Vieja de Pollo

One of the most iconic dishes from Cuba, Ropa Vieja means old clothes. It came to Cuba from Spain, from the Sepharadic recipes, and really became a staple of Latin cooking. The authentic Ropa Vieja is made with meat, garlic, onions, bell peppers, spices, olives, capers, and herbs. The meat is then simmered and braised until completely soft and falling apart. Then it's shredded and mixed back into the sauce. In my eternal quest to healthify things, I prepare Ropa Vieja with chicken. It shreds beautifully, Cuban style, flashy, rich, and unapologetically decadent—with a Latina cook behind it. Let's start calling this dish "Ropa Nueva," or new clothes, shall we? **Serves 4 to 6**

2 pounds chicken thighs, skin on

Kosher salt and freshly ground black pepper

2 tablespoons extra-virgin olive oil

3 cloves garlic

1 onion, sliced

1 red bell pepper, sliced

1 green bell pepper, sliced

1 teaspoon cumin

1 teaspoon coriander

1 teaspoon oregano

½ teaspoon Spanish paprika

¼ teaspoon freshly ground nutmeg

1 tablespoon tomato paste

1 (16-ounce) can whole peeled tomatoes, crushed

¼ cup dry white wine

2 cups chicken stock

½ cup pitted green olives

2 tablespoons capers

¼ cup freshly chopped parsley

1. **Cook the Chicken:** Spread chicken over a sheet pan covered with paper towels and pat dry. Season with freshly ground pepper on both sides.

2. In a large heavy pot (at least 12 inches wide) over medium heat, pour the olive oil, and cook the chicken skin side down until lightly browned all over, about 3 minutes per side. Using a slotted spoon transfer chicken to a bowl and cover with foil to keep moist.

3. **Cook the Vegetables:** Using the fat that's left in the pan (if there is too much fat, drain a little), reduce the heat to low, add the garlic, and cook until it just starts to turn golden, about 1 minute. Add the onion and peppers, season lightly with salt and pepper and cook, stirring frequently with a wooden spoon, until vegetables are soft and translucent, about 4 minutes.

4. Add the cumin, coriander, oregano, paprika, and nutmeg and continue cooking until fragrant.

5. Add the tomato paste and crushed tomatoes and continue cooking on low heat.

6. Add the wine and cook until almost completely evaporated, about 3 minutes.

7. Return the chicken back to the pot, add any juices accumulated in the bowl, and surround the chicken with the vegetables, simmering on low heat just with the moisture of the vegetables for a few minutes.

(Continued on next page)

8. Pour the chicken stock in, cover the pan, and braise the chicken gently for 1 hour on low heat, checking occasionally to make sure liquid level is not too dry. If it seems like there is too much liquid at first, don't worry, the chicken and vegetables will absorb during braising and shredding time.

9. After one hour, chicken meat should be falling off the bones. Uncover the pan, remove the chicken thighs, and let them cool to the touch, about 5 minutes.

10. Shred the Chicken: Separate the chicken meat from skin, fat, and bones (discard the fat, and reserve bones to make chicken stock), and shred the chicken meat into thin threads, discarding any undesired veiny pieces. Return the meat to the sauce, and cook again, simmering gently until the sauce thickens but looks incredibly moist and rich, about 20 minutes.

11. Add the olives, capers, and parsley, and mix well. Serve hot with a side of yellow rice or brown rice, or any other healthy grain of your choice.

Warm Cucumber Chicken Salad

I believe that cooking is an art with potent power, like language, music, or literature. It has the power to lift, communicate, transform, and nourish. That's how I feel when see the creativity going on in South America. Once I was in Santiago de Chile and ate a warm cucumber salad with chicken. Cucumber is such a staple ingredient in South America, in fact, all over the world, but it never crossed my mind to apply it this way. And it was so simple, but I couldn't get the flavors out of my head! I instinctively re-created the recipe, adding queso-blanco and dill. If you have feta cheese in your fridge, by all means, use it. If you have goat cheese, that's fine too. **Serves 3**

1 pound boneless, skinless chicken breasts

Kosher salt and freshly ground pepper

3 tablespoons olive oil

1 small shallot, finely chopped

1 cucumber, seeded, half peeled, and chopped

$\frac{1}{4}$ cup chopped freshly chopped dill

$\frac{1}{4}$ pound *queso-blanco* (or feta cheese)

1. Season the chicken with salt and pepper on both sides. In a medium pan, warm 2 tablespoons olive oil and cook the chicken until golden brown and cooked all through, about 4 minutes on each side. Place on a plate and cover to rest.

2. To the same pan, add the shallot, and cook over low heat, until soft, about 2 minutes. Add the cucumber and cook ever so slightly, until cucumber is starting to soften but still crispy.

3. Chop chicken into $\frac{1}{2}$-inch cubes, place in a bowl with the cucumber, dill, and season with salt and pepper.

4. Add the cheese and carefully toss with the chicken and cucumber, making sure the cheese stays in chunks. Serve immediately.

Turkey Sausage with Bell Peppers

There was a time in my life, when I was just out cooking school, that uncomplicated cooking was simply not of interest to me. In fact, I would prefer my work to be uneasy. These days, I am cooking for total health. For people. For life. How I like to cook: I just love using bell peppers, tomatoes, onions, and garlic. Add some sausage and the taste that builds up goes from plain to plain wonderful! Mamita! *Make that for dinner, with a sip of wine and a good tortilla on the side, and the morning will become bright and filled with possibilities. Eat the leftovers for lunch, and there is no nap required. Much of the cooking can be done ahead of time.* **Serves 4**

2 tablespoons extra-virgin olive oil

1¼ pounds turkey sausage (about 8 links)

3 cloves garlic, finely minced

1 onion, thinly sliced

1 red bell pepper, seeded and thinly sliced

1 green bell pepper, seeded and thinly sliced

1 yellow bell pepper, seeded and thinly sliced

Kosher salt and freshly ground black pepper

½ teaspoon paprika

1 teaspoon dried oregano

¼ teaspoon freshly ground nutmeg

¼ cup white wine

1¼ cups chicken stock

¼ cup freshly chopped parsley

1. In a large deep pan, warm the olive oil over medium heat. Add the sausage and brown them on all sides until golden brown, about 8 minutes. Remove from the pan and place in a bowl or plate; cover with foil to keep moist.

2. Since you are using chicken sausage, there shouldn't be too much fat left in the pan, but just enough to cook the garlic, on very low heat, stirring with a wooden spoon, until it just starts to turn golden, about 2 minutes (if there is excessive fat in the fat in the pan, remove with a spoon and discard).

3. Add the onion and bell peppers at the same time. Season lightly with salt and pepper and cook, stirring frequently with a wooden spoon.

4. Add the paprika, oregano, and nutmeg and continue cooking, until the vegetables are soft and tender, stirring often, about 5 minutes.

5. Add the white wine and let it evaporate completely.

6. Add the chicken stock and bring to a boil over high heat. Turn the heat to low and return the sausage links to the pan, along with any accumulated juices on the bottom of the pan. Taste the sauce and adjust the seasoning if necessary. Cover the pan and simmer on low heat for 20 minutes, until the dish becomes one.

7. Uncover the pan and simmer for another 5 minutes still on low heat. Garnish with parsley and serve hot.

Chicken Tamale Pie

As a cookbook author, I'm faced with an occupational hazard: cooking. As the spokesperson of a lifestyle campaign I provide healthy recipes—this means more cooking! Cooking, for me, is the greatest way to get complete control of your health. And it helps me focus more—not less—on the things I love the most: food and cooking. My approach to cooking is not about this diet or that diet. It's about a long-term eating plan that involves home cooking. Next Sunday, when you devote a few hours to cook for the week, is the perfect time to make this recipe. You might even want to consider doubling, as it freezes very well.

Every cuisine has a name for its version of Shepherd's Pie. In Brazil we call it Escondidinho, in Argentina we call it Pastel, in America we call it Shepherd's Pie. I am calling this recipe Chicken Tamale Pie, because the meat layer is prepared with a mixture of ground chicken and turkey (though it's okay to stick to one or another) and the upper crust is prepared with fresh corn or a corn soufflé as I used to eat in as a child in Rio. Cook it with love. Have your children taste the meat layer while it's cooking; better yet, invite them to cook with you. Cooking is an education. Not only for health but for life. It forces you to think about what you're eating before you buy the ingredients. It makes you think while you're preparing a recipe. It teaches you math, organization skills, and life skills. And it helps you utilize one of the most valuable tools in the kitchen: your brain. **Serves 6 to 8**

For the Meat Layer:

2 tablespoons olive oil
2 cloves garlic, chopped
½ cup chopped onion, about 1 small onion
½ cup chopped scallions, about 2
½ cup chopped carrots, about 1 small carrot
½ cup chopped celery, about 2 stalks
5 plum tomatoes, peeled, seeded, and roughly chopped
1¼ pounds ground chicken and/or turkey
1 (6-ounce) can tomato paste
⅓ cup white wine
1 cup fat-free milk
1 cup water
Kosher salt and freshly ground pepper
Freshly ground nutmeg

Equipment: 7 x 11 baking dish

Prepare the Meat Layer:

1. Pour the olive oil in a large, heavy bottomed saucepan over medium heat and cook the garlic, until just golden brown, about 3 minutes.

2. Add the onions, scallions, carrots, and celery, and cook, stirring frequently, until the vegetables are soft and tender, about 3 minutes.

3. Add the tomatoes, and cook, stirring occasionally, until they get soft and mushy.

4. Add the ground chicken and turkey and, using the wooden spoon, break into tiny bits until completely cooked through, about 6 to 8 minutes.

5. Add the tomato paste and mix well.

6. Add the wine and reduce by half, about 3 minutes.

7. Add the milk and water. Stir gently and cook, partly covered, for 30 minutes over low heat.

(Continued on page 121)

½ teaspoon paprika

½ teaspoon ground coriander

2 tablespoons chopped fresh
 parsley

For the Corn Layer:

4 tablespoons unsalted butter,
 melted

3 cups corn kernels (fresh or
 frozen)

3 eggs, separated

Kosher salt and freshly ground
 pepper

Freshly ground nutmeg

¾ cup Parmesan

8. Season with salt, pepper, nutmeg, paprika, and coriander to taste and finish with the fresh parsley. Transfer sauce to the baking dish, spread with a spatula, and cool to room temperature.

Prepare the Corn Topping:

1. Preheat the oven to 375°F.

2. Place the butter in a food processor with the corn, egg yolks, salt, pepper, nutmeg, and ½ cup of the Parmesan. Pulse to combine.

3. In the bowl of an electric mixer, beat the egg whites until stiff. Fold gently into the corn mixture. The egg whites will not puff the corn mixture too much. Gently pour the corn mixture over the turkey/chicken layer and spread with a spatula. Scatter the remaining ½ cup Parmesan cheese on top. Bake the pie in the oven, rotating once during baking time until nicely golden brown, about 25 minutes. Be careful not to let it get too brown. Remove from the oven and let it rest for 10 minutes before serving.

For the corn kernels, you can use either fresh, frozen, or canned corn.

If you use fresh corn, you will need about 4 to5 ears of corn. Cook them first (simply place them in a pot, cover with cold water, and bring to a boil, cooking for 5 to 8 minutes) then cut the kernels off the cob with a sharp knife using a sawing motion over a bowl. Discard the cob.

If you use frozen corn, make sure to let it come to room temperature.

If you use canned corn, make sure to drain the water. An 8-ounce can will yield 1 cup of corn kernels.

Chicken in a Pot

While I have not yet visited Portugal, I already know I feel right at home. That's because I'm a daughter of Rio, probably one of the most Portuguese towns in all of Brazil. Portugal colonized Brazil, and Brazilian culture is a mixture of three different influences: the Portuguese, the African, and the native Indian. But in certain parts of the country you'll find one influence stronger than others, and in Rio, my friends, it's all about Portugal. Travel north to Bahia, and you're in Africa. Take a slight turn to the left/north and you're at the heart of Amazon with all the bright native indigenous culture. All the Lusitan flavors, the cod fish, garlic, pastries, blue china, embroidery, and the nuns, are part of my culture. Frango na Púcara is one of those dishes: classic, iconic, and delicious. I make Frango na Púcara in my American kitchen quite often and my kids love it. **Serves 6**

1 whole chicken (about
   3½ pounds), broken down
Kosher salt and freshly ground
   pepper
2 tablespoons olive oil
2 medium onions, sliced
4 cloves garlic, minced
2 bay leaves
1 (28-ounce) can whole peeled
   tomatoes, preferably San
   Marzano, drained, half
   the juice reserved, and
   chopped
⅓ cup golden raisins
½ cup port wine
½ cup dry white wine
1 tablespoon Dijon mustard
3 tablespoons freshly
   chopped parsley

1. Season chicken with salt and pepper all over. Heat the oil in a large pot over medium-high heat. Working in batches, sear the pieces, skin side down, until golden brown, about 4 minutes per side. Transfer pieces to a bowl and cover with foil to keep moist.

2. Drain off all but a thin film of oil from the pot (if the pot is dry, add more oil). Reduce heat to low, add the onions, and cook until soft, about 5 minutes. Add the garlic and cook for 2 minutes more. Add the bay leaves. Add the tomatoes and their juices and cook until it all starts to get mushy and bubbly.

3. Return the chicken to the pan and throw in the raisins.

4. In a small bowl whisk together the port, white wine, and mustard; pour over the chicken. Bring to a boil, reduce the heat to low and simmer, covered, turning the pieces to keep them submerged, until the chicken is cooked through and very tender, about 45 to 60 minutes.

5. To serve, arrange the chicken in the middle of a platter and surround with the onions and raisins. Pour sauce all over and serve hot. Garnish with parsley.

Chicken Barley Stew

Being Jewish, Brazilian, Moroccan, Latina, and now American, sometimes I think that I hit the cultural food jackpot. Shabbat in Rio de Janeiro is the kind of thing that didn't match, and it's exactly how I grew up: samba, carnival—and gefilte fish! Rio de Janeiro in the 1980s and 1990s was a hotbed of Brazilian radicalism; inflation, violence, and corruption on one hand; Judaism, Hebrew, and Israeli dancing on the other. All mixed, all scrambled like one big omelet, and very much part of my life.

And then there was food. A lot happened during Shabbat dinners, which was not like any dinner. It mattered more than any other night, because the stories that were told with the foods we ate are the backbone of my family's history. Like my grandmother's chicken stew, which was served at many Shabbats.

Over chicken stew, Vovó Estella (my grandmother) would tell me about her escape from Morocco, the foods she had to eat to survive, and those she dreamed about eating. She grew up in Tangier and had five kids. They came to Rio in the 1960s. She spoke Spanish and nothing else. I've been making this dish for a long time. It brings great memories of my grandmother. Today, I speak Spanish just like her, in a singing tone and with a smile on my face. **Serves 6 to 8**

1 cup pearl barley
8 skinless chicken thighs, bone-in
Kosher salt and freshly ground pepper
2 tablespoons olive oil
2 cloves garlic, minced
1 tablespoon oregano
Pinch ground nutmeg
1 large white onion, finely chopped
4 plum tomatoes, skinned, seeded, and chopped
¼ teaspoon paprika
2 pounds cremini mushrooms, quartered
1½ cups chicken broth
A few sprigs thyme for garnish

1. Bring a large pot of water to a boil. Add salt and barley and partially cover. Cook over medium heat until barley is nice and tender, about 35 minutes. Drain over a colander and discard the water.

2. Season the chicken with salt and pepper on both sides.

3. In a large braising pan (with deep sides) warm the olive oil over medium-high heat. Add the chicken pieces and cook until nicely golden brown, about 5 minutes on each side. Remove the chicken thighs into a bowl and cover with aluminum foil to keep moist.

4. Lower the heat, add the garlic, and cook, stirring constantly with a wooden spoon, until it just begins to turn golden.

5. Add the oregano and nutmeg and stir.

6. Add the onion, stirring frequently with a wooden spoon until everything is soft and translucent. Season lightly with salt and pepper.

7. Add the tomatoes and paprika and continue cooking until everything smells delicious and it looks like a gorgeous *sofrito*.

8. Add the mushrooms and cook until soft, about 5 minutes, stirring frequently.

9. Add the chicken and any accumulated juices and mix, very carefully, everything on the pan so that flavors can meld together, for 5 minutes.

10. Add the broth and bring to a boil. At this point you want to taste and adjust seasoning. Cover the pan and simmer very gently over low heat for a good 20 minutes.

11. Add the barley, mix carefully with a wooden spoon, and continue cooking for another 20 minutes. Garnish with thyme, divide into plates, and serve hot.

Chicken, Cashew, and Red Pepper Stir Fry

São Paulo's late 1980s fusion of Japanese and Brazilian cuisines created a culture of blending that persists today, even as the world around us changes constantly. Is it any surprise that me, a Latina chef, is blending Japanese, Brazilian, and American ingredients in my recipes? Welcome to my kitchen!

Here, I highlight Asian cooking and how it's being adapted, rethought, and remade for this generation, transforming a simple healthy recipe into a healthy body and mind. There is nothing fancy about this stir fry, and that's the point. A stir fry is about as unassuming as food can get, but when done well, it packs more flavor and more soul per square inch than anything else this humble. The ingredients are standard: chicken, garlic, ginger, scallions, red bell peppers, and cashews. All common to Japanese and Brazilian cuisines alike. It's prepared for us to cook and enjoy, taste, and repeat. **Serves 4**

1⅓ pounds boneless, skinless chicken breasts
Kosher salt
Freshly ground pepper
3 tablespoons olive oil
1 tablespoon sesame oil
3 cloves garlic, finely mined
1 teaspoon grated ginger
1 onion, thinly sliced
1 red pepper, seeded, thinly sliced
4 scallions, white and green parts, chopped on a bias
1 cup chicken broth
1½ tablespoons soy sauce
1 teaspoon cornstarch
½ teaspoon organic cane sugar
½ cup cashews
½ cup freshly chopped chives

1. Pat chicken dry and cut breasts into strips ¼- to ½-inch thick. Season with salt and pepper.

2. Warm 2 tablespoons of the olive oil on a wok or a 12-inch skillet over high heat, and cook the chicken, in batches if necessary, until all pieces are just cooked through, about 4 minutes per batch. Transfer each batch to a bowl and cover with foil.

3. Add the remaining 1 tablespoon olive oil and the sesame oil; add the garlic and ginger, reduce the heat to low, and cook until it just starts to turn golden, about 2 minutes (since the pan will already be hot from cooking the chicken, it tends to burn easily, so pay attention).

4. Add the onion, red pepper, and scallions and cook, stirring occasionally with a wooden spoon, until vegetables are tender, about 5 minutes. Season lightly with salt and pepper.

5. Pour the chicken broth and bring to a boil.

6. In a small bowl, whisk together the soy sauce, cornstarch, and sugar. Reduce the heat to low and add cornstarch mixture to the pan. Cook slowly until the sauce thickens.

7. Return the chicken (add any accumulated juices) and cook for another 3 to 5 minutes until everything blends together.

8. Stir in the cashews and chives, mixing them into the sauce. Serve over healthy grains such as brown rice or quinoa, or any other grain of your preference.

Chicken with Peas and Potatoes

The older I get, the more and more I get into healthy cooking. Not that I wasn't into it before, but let's be honest, as we get older, we simply cannot eat the same things we could when we were teenagers or young adults. At the same time, I'm a mother to two amazing teenagers who love to eat, love my cooking, and are hungry all the time! One of the biggest pleasures of life is making dinner for my family. From the days my kids were very young, I always made healthy recipes that can be served for the whole family. But it's quite interesting . . . when they were younger, they didn't appreciate food to the fullest. As they became teenagers and started to eat at their friend's houses, that's when they realized that home cooking was a lot better than anything else! This recipe is one of their favorites: chicken, peas, and potatoes. A healthy dish, full of flavor and ready to feed my hungry kids. Depending on the size of the chicken breasts, you may want to cut thin slices. For the potatoes, I like the red skin potatoes as it adds a nice color, but you could use Yukon gold potatoes. This reheats very well. **Serves 4**

¼ cup flour
Kosher salt and freshly ground
    black pepper
2 boneless skinless chicken
    breasts, cut in half horizontally
    and trimmed
5 teaspoons olive oil
12 ounces red potatoes
    (unpeeled), washed, and cut
    into 1-inch pieces
1 clove garlic, minced
1 shallot, finely sliced
1 teaspoon dried oregano
¼ cup dry white wine
1 cup chicken broth
½ cup frozen peas, thawed
¼ cup freshly chopped parsley

1. Place flour in a shallow dish, and season with salt and pepper.

2. Pat chicken dry and season with salt and pepper. Dredge chicken in flour and shake off the excess.

3. In a large nonstick skillet, heat 2 teaspoons olive oil over medium heat. Add the chicken and cook until they just begin to turn golden brown on each side, about 3 to 4 minutes per side. Transfer to a plate and cover with foil to keep moist.

4. Heat 2 teaspoons olive oil in the pan and add the potatoes. Cook, stirring occasionally until they are tender but not soft, about 7 minutes.

5. Remove the potatoes to the same pan as the chicken and keep them covered.

6. Add the remaining 1 teaspoon olive oil and garlic, and cook until it just starts to turn golden, about 1 minute.

7. Add the shallot and cook until translucent. Add the oregano and season with salt and pepper.

8. Add the white wine, bring to a boil, and reduce.

9. Add the chicken broth and bring to a boil.

(Continued on next page)

10. Reduce the heat, return the chicken and potatoes to the pan, cover, and simmer gently until the potatoes are completely cooked and the chicken is tender, about 10 minutes.

11. Remove the lid, and add the peas, cooking everything together for another 3 to 5 minutes. Taste and be sure to adjust the seasoning.

12. Garnish with parsley and serve on a rimmed plate, spooning the sauce over the chicken.

Turkey with Mole Sauce

Moles hold a very high esteem in Mexican cooking. I'm surprised that it never acquired the same esteem on other countries of Latin America. As a Brazilian, I can tell you that it might be because most moles are way too spicy. Even in the Bahia region, where hot peppers are quite common, we don't see mole sauce. As an American, I feel that mole has a reputation for being very complex and elaborated to prepare, making a lot of people feel intimidated to cook it at home. But this is an incredibly rich sauce that can be calibrated to your own liking and simplified in preparation. And that's exactly what I did in this recipe, in a way that's approachable and doable in any kitchen. In my own interpretation, mole becomes a tomato sauce that's enhanced with lots of ingredients, such as dried peppers, nuts, spices, dried fruits, chocolate, and liquid. Think of it as a tomato sauce elevated to the fifth potential. It's traditional to serve mole with chicken, pork, or turkey. In my version, I prepare it with chili powder (instead of steaming, seeding, and roasting dried chiles), peanut butter, which adds a nice creamy texture, raisins, and cocoa powder. If you've never tried making mole at home, I hope this recipe will inspire you. It's quite easy to follow. Feel free to use as little or as much chili powder as you like. Really, this is the only ingredient that needs calibration. Everything else, you can follow through. I often see turkey tenderloins, which are nice and lean, but feel free to use turkey breast or chicken breast. Roast in the oven until it's perfectly tender and juicy. Here is a winning dish, that hopefully you can incorporate to your regular repertoire when you're looking for something interesting to do with chicken or turkey. You'll be saying Holy Mole with a smile on your face! **Serves 4**

For the Turkey:
1½ pounds turkey tenderloins (or 1 bone-in turkey breast)
Kosher salt and freshly ground pepper
4 tablespoons olive oil

For the Mole Sauce:
2 tablespoons olive oil
3 cloves garlic, minced
1 large onion, chopped
5 plum tomatoes, peeled, seeded, and roughly chopped
2 sprigs rosemary
1 bay leaf
1–2 tablespoons chili powder (start with one and you can always add more)
2 tablespoons unsweetened cocoa powder

1. **Roast the Turkey:** Preheat the oven to 375°F. Arrange turkey in a baking dish and season with salt and pepper on both sides. Brush the olive all over and roast in the oven until it's perfectly cooked, about 30 to 35 minutes.

2. **Prepare the Mole Sauce:** In a saucepan, add the olive oil and cook the garlic over medium heat until it just starts to turn golden, about 2 minutes. Add the onion and cook, mixing occasionally with a wooden spoon, until nice and translucent, about 5 minutes.

3. Add the tomatoes and let them get hot.

4. Add the rosemary, bay leaf, chili powder, cocoa powder, cinnamon, raisins, peanut butter, and orange juice. Cook everything together until it just starts to combine, about 5 minutes.

5. Add chicken stock and simmer over medium heat, stirring occasionally until the sauce is slightly thickened, about 10 minutes. Taste and adjust the seasoning.

(Continued on page 131)

½ teaspoon ground cinnamon

½ cup raisins

2 tablespoons creamy peanut butter

¼ cup freshly squeezed orange juice (about 1 orange)

1½ cups chicken stock

2 tablespoons sesame seeds for garnish

6. Discard the rosemary and bay leaf and transfer the sauce to a blender. Puree until smooth and transfer to a bowl. Sauce can be done 5 days ahead of time. You will have extra sauce, which freezes very well.

7. Remove the turkey from the oven and transfer to a cutting board. Generously spoon the sauce all over the breast. Cut the turkey into slices, about ½-inch thick, and fan them out into a nice serving platter. Add a little more mole to the platter and sprinkle sesame seeds on top.

Coffee-Rubbed Chicken Breast with Corn Salsa

This smoky coffee rub adds a lovely touch to the chicken breast and changes the whole flavor profile of this dish. You can make this coffee rub in batches and store in a mason jar and it will stay for months in your spice cabinet. It's a great starting point for grilling season. And who doesn't love that crispy char on chicken breasts? The corn salsa is quite refreshing and goes well with many dishes. **Serves 4**

For the Coffee Rub:

2 tablespoons finely ground dark roast coffee beans
2 tablespoons chile powder
1 tablespoon smoked paprika
1½ teaspoons ground coriander
1 tablespoon kosher salt
4 boneless skinless chicken breasts
2 tablespoons olive oil

For the Corn Salsa:

1 teaspoon minced garlic (about 1 clove)
1 shallot, minced
2 tablespoons freshly squeezed lemon juice
½ cup extra-virgin olive oil
2 cups cooked corn kernels
1 red bell pepper, diced (about 1 cup)
Kosher salt and freshly ground pepper
2 tablespoons freshly chopped chives
1 tablespoon freshly chopped cilantro

1. In a small bowl, combine the coffee, chile powder, paprika, coriander, and kosher salt.

2. Rub the coffee mixture all over the chicken on both sides and let sit at room temperature for 30 minutes.

3. Heat the grill on medium high and oil the grates.

4. Carefully brush the olive oil over the chicken breast and grill them until fully opaque with no traces of pink (take a peek by removing one breast and nick with a knife), about 5 minutes per side.

5. For the corn salsa: In a medium bowl mix the garlic, shallot, and lemon juice.

6. Slowly add the olive oil, whisking all the while until it thickens.

7. In another bowl place the corn, red bell pepper, and herbs, and mix well. Pour the sauce over and fold everything together. Taste and season with salt and pepper. Serve with the chicken breasts.

> Chili powder is different than chile powder.
> Chili powder refers to a blend of ground dried chile peppers mixed with other spices like cumin, peppercorn, and salt. Chile powder refers to a single chile ingredient.

Grilled Chicken Drumstick with Orange Glaze

This recipe can be dinner tomorrow night, with a light breeze over the backyard, a beautiful table setting, and wine poured in each glass as friends sit around to enjoy. A blond orange honey glaze sits on top of the moist, fragrant chicken, and juices run thick to pool beneath it, a kind of syrup, delicious in its intensity. It is chicken glaze glory. Feel free to use drumsticks, thighs, or both. **Serves 4**

Zest from 1 orange
1 cup freshly squeezed orange
 juice
1 cup white wine
1 ounce fresh ginger, thinly
 sliced
3 tablespoons honey
8 chicken drumsticks (about
 2 pounds total)
Kosher salt and freshly ground
 black pepper
3 tablespoons extra-virgin
 olive oil
3 tablespoons fresh chopped
 cilantro

1. In a medium saucepan, combine the orange zest, juice, wine, ginger, and honey, and bring to boil on high heat. Reduce the heat so the mixture simmers gently and cook until it starts to take on a syrup consistency, 18 to 20 minutes. Strain through a fine sieve and cool completely. You should have between ¾ and 1 cup. You can prepare the glaze up to 3 days ahead of time and keep in a covered container in the refrigerator.

2. Bring the chicken to room temperature before cooking. Season the chicken with salt and pepper on both sides and moisten with olive oil all over.

3. Heat your grill to high and oil with cooking spray.

4. Put the chicken on the grill and cook until the skin starts to get crispy, about 8 minutes. If fat drips into the fire and causes it to flame, move the chicken around so they are not directly over the flames. Or you can also use a small spritz water bottle to contain the flames. Turn the chicken and continue to cook until the thickest part of the drumstick is no longer red, about another 8 minutes.

5. During the last minute of cooking, brush the chicken deliberately with the orange glaze all over.

6. Transfer to a plate, and brush again with the glaze; sprinkle with freshly chopped cilantro and serve hot.

Chicken Stew with Tomatillos and Cilantro

This recipe is for one of those nights when everyone gathers around the kitchen, curiosity afoot, one person starts asking about tomatillos (that would be my son, Thomas) and another asks about chicken stock (that would be my daughter, Bianca). They come closer to the stove, and everyone is just waiting to savor the food being prepared.

As I tell them, tomatillo is an important ingredient in the Latin kitchen. They are a beautiful fruit with the husk on top and a slight wax on the outside, but it's almost impossible to eat raw. Rather, the beauty is that its flavors provide acidity and herbal nuances to sauces and stews. Be sure to always remove the husks and rinse them well over tepid water to remove any excess stickiness.

Bianca is crazy for all things chicken soup, so she often sees me making homemade chicken stock, which I firmly believe is it one of the biggest differences between restaurant cooking and home cooking. I simply save the bones of a roasted chicken, throw them in a pot with cold water, and simmer for about 40 minutes.

Serves 8

3 cups chicken stock

1 pound tomatillos, husked, rinsed, cut into ½-inch wedges

1 bunch scallions, coarsely chopped

1½ cups packed fresh cilantro (reserve a few leaves for garnish)

3 cloves garlic, roughly chopped

3 tablespoons olive oil

4 pounds boneless skinless chicken breast, cut into 1-inch cubes

Kosher salt, freshly ground pepper

1 large onion, chopped

½ teaspoon cumin seeds

½ teaspoon ground coriander

2 teaspoons dry oregano

1½ pounds small young potatoes, peeled, cut in half

Sweet drop miniature red peppers to garnish

1. In a blender, combine 2 cups chicken broth, ¼ of the tomatillos, and the scallions, cilantro, and garlic in a blender. Set the *salsa verde* aside.

2. Heat a heavy large pan and add oil; season chicken with salt and pepper. Working in batches, add the chicken and sear on all sides, turning occasionally, about 4 minutes per batch. Using a slotted spoon, transfer to a bowl and cover with aluminum foil to keep moist.

3. If there is too much fat left in the pan, remove some. If there is too little fat, add some oil. Add the onion and reduce the heat to low. Season lightly with salt and pepper and cook until soft and translucent, stirring occasionally with a wooden spoon, about 5 minutes.

4. Add the cumin and cook until it starts to develop flavor, about 2 minutes. Add the remaining tomatillos and cook everything together until tender, about 5 minutes. Return the chicken and any juices that accumulated in the bowl to the pot, add 2 cups of the *salsa verde*, the remaining 1 cup of chicken stock, and oregano. Season everything with salt and pepper. Cover and cook gently and slowly over low heat until the chicken is tender, about 45 minutes.

5. Add potatoes to the chicken and simmer until they are just tender, about 20 minutes. Stir in the remaining *salsa verde*. If necessary, thin with a little more broth. Check seasoning again and divide among hot bowls. Garnish with sweet drop peppers and cilantro leaves.

Picadillo de Pollo

I am not sure if we can still assume that winter will bring the cold temps, but Sundays still have a cozy feeling in the air that makes me want to spend time in the kitchen. What nicer way to spend a Sunday afternoon slowly simmering this Picadillo de Pollo (picadillo means "chopped small"), a "meaty" ragú that will taste even better the following week? And did I mention that it freezes beautiful for that Sunday you'll be out the whole day?

That's right, this Picadillo de Pollo is a thick sauce of minced vegetables, ground chicken, wine, and tomato paste, and depending on whose abuelita *you ask, tomatoes, and is a staple of Latin cooking. Time is your great ally here; this dish is all about cooking low and slow, until the picadillo looks thick, like a meat pudding. Once the active part of chopping and cooking is done, set the pot on the lowest setting and the rest of the afternoon is yours—which in my case, I'll be thinking about what to cook the following Sunday!*

Serves 4 to 6

4 tablespoons extra-virgin olive oil

2 pounds ground chicken or turkey

Kosher salt and freshly ground pepper

3 cloves garlic, minced

1 onion, chopped

1 red bell pepper, seeded and chopped

3 scallions, white and green parts, chopped

2 celery stalks, chopped

1 carrot, peeled and roughly chopped

1 pound (about 4) plum tomatoes, peeled, seeded, and chopped

1 tablespoon dried oregano

Freshly grated nutmeg

1 teaspoon paprika

½ teaspoon coriander

¼ teaspoon ground chili pepper

½ cup white wine

1 tablespoon tomato paste

1 cup water

1½ cups chicken stock

½ cup freshly chopped parsley

½ cup freshly chopped cilantro

1. Heat 2 tablespoons of the oil in a large heavy-bottomed saucepan over high heat.

2. Season the ground chicken with salt and pepper. Add the chicken to the pan and cook it until the moisture evaporates and the meat is cooked through. Transfer to a bowl and cover with foil to keep moist.

3. Place the remaining olive oil in the same pan, reduce the heat to low, and add the garlic. Cook until it just starts to turn golden, about 2 minutes. Add the onion, pepper, scallions, celery, and carrot. Cook, stirring frequently, until the vegetables become soft and tender and absorb all the brown bits in the pan.

4. Add the tomatoes, and cook until mushy, about 4 minutes.

5. Season lightly with salt and pepper, oregano, nutmeg, paprika, coriander, and chili pepper.

6. Return the chicken and all accumulated juices to the pan and stir.

7. Add the white wine, tomato paste, water, and chicken stock. Cover the pot and turn the heat very low and simmer for 45 to 60 minutes, checking occasionally on the liquid level. If it looks dry, feel free to add some more liquid (chicken stock or water). Look for a sauce that is wet enough without being extremely brothy. Taste the dish and adjust the seasoning.

8. Serve the *picadillo* over brown rice, or another side of your choice, and garnish with fresh parsley and cilantro.

Roasted Chicken Breast with Guava BBQ Sauce

Many gastronomes consider chicken breast boring. Not me. I love it; I see it as a blank slate, and if you want to make your chicken breast sing, I have the recipe for you. What makes it sing? The contrast of sweet and savory flavors. This chicken breast roasts pure and clean beneath a big flavored guava sauce. Choose a guava paste that is not too sweet. If you can't find guava paste, quince paste will do. This recipe would be nice on the grill as well (start with the chicken marinating in a bit of the guava sauce and brush more sauce right on the grill). As long as you don't overcook it—perhaps the single reason most people associate chicken breast with boring—you can hear some loud Latin music in your kitchen! **Serves 4**

For the Guava Sauce:

2 tablespoons extra-virgin olive oil
4 cloves garlic, crushed and
    roughly chopped
1 large onion, roughly chopped
2–3 bay leaves
2 sprigs rosemary
$1/3$ cup soy sauce
$1/2$ cup guava paste

For the Chicken:

4 boneless, skinless chicken
    breasts, trimmed of excess fat,
    rinsed, and patted dry
Kosher salt and freshly ground
    black pepper
1 tablespoon olive oil
1 tablespoon white wine
Parsley or any herb for garnish

Make the Guava Sauce:

1. In a medium saucepan, warm the olive oil over medium heat. Add garlic and cook slowly over low heat until it just starts to turn golden. Add the onion, bay leaves, and rosemary and cook until everything is blended, soft, and translucent, about 4 minutes.

2. Add the soy sauce and bring to a boil. Add the guava paste and mix well until dissolved. Cover the pan; simmer the sauce on low heat until slightly thickened, 7 to 10 minutes. Remove the bay leaves and rosemary. Transfer the sauce to a food processor and puree until smooth. Pour into a bowl and let it cool completely. Guava sauce can be done up to 5 days ahead of time.

Cook the Chicken:

1. Place the chicken in a zip-top bag, season with salt and pepper, and add about $1/4$ cup of the guava sauce. Massage well, making sure the chicken is completely covered in the sauce. Marinate at room temperature for 30 minutes or up to 1 day ahead, if kept in the refrigerator.

2. Bring the chicken to room temperature at least 30 minutes before cooking.

3. Preheat the oven to 375˚F. Spread the chicken on a roasting pan or casserole baking dish, add the olive

oil and white wine and roast for 15 minutes, uncovered. Remove from the oven, brush on a heavy coating of guava sauce, and roast again until the chicken breast is nicely brown, about 15 minutes more. Garnish with parsley and serve hot.

Braised Chicken with Fennel and Oranges

My friend Sheila Neilinger, born and raised in São Paulo, is the kind of person who claims (wrongly) she doesn't know how to cook. Yet, she is a terrific host. We have celebrated many dinners together with our families. One day, she invited us over and served this amazing Braised Chicken with Fennel and Oranges. I couldn't resist but asking her for the recipe; she explained that she braises the chicken separately from the fennel and oranges and brings them together at the end of the cooking process. I took the cue and developed a recipe with her directions in mind. There is no question that she knows how to cook! **Serves 4**

8 chicken thighs (about
   3 pounds), skin on
Kosher salt and freshly ground
   pepper
2 tablespoons olive oil
2 medium fennel bulbs, cut
   in half lengthwise and
   quartered
2 small onions, peeled and cut
   in half
4 navel oranges, sliced into
   ¼-inch rounds
3 cloves garlic, minced
3 tablespoons freshly
   squeezed orange juice
1 cup chicken stock

1. Preheat the oven to 325°F. Season the chicken with salt and pepper on both sides.

2. Pour the olive oil into a large and deep sauté pan (about 12 inches diameter) over medium heat. Add the chicken thighs skin side down and cook until nicely golden brown on both sides, about 3 minutes per side.

3. Transfer the chicken to a clean bowl and cover with aluminum foil to keep moist.

4. Add a bit more oil to the pan if necessary. Add the fennel quarters (facing down) and onion, half facing down, and brown until they look nice and golden on the flat side. Turn fennel and onions and cook on the other side until just starting to turn golden, about 3 minutes. Transfer vegetables to a flat tray and cover lightly with foil.

5. Add the oranges, and brown them lightly on both sides until they begin to caramelize, about 2 minutes per side. Transfer to the tray with vegetables. Cover again with foil.

6. Make sure there is enough oil in the pan, and add the garlic and cook until it just starts to turn golden, about 1 minute.

7. Deglaze the pan with orange juice and let it come to a boil.

8. Add the chicken stock and bring to a boil. Reduce the heat and add the chicken thighs back to the pan, nestling them so they are half-covered with liquid. Cover the pan and bake in the oven for 45 minutes, until the chicken is soft.

9. Remove the pan from the oven, add the fennel, onions, and oranges, cover the pan again and braise in the oven for another 40 minutes.

10. Spoon the chicken, fennel, oranges, and onions into a serving platter. Pour the cooking liquid all over. Garnish with some fennel tops.

Quinoa with Chicken Sausage and Mushrooms

Not too long ago, quinoa was a completely obscure ingredient. People didn't even know how to pronounce it (it's keen-wah). Certainly, home cooks didn't know how to use it and only die-hard vegan restaurants would serve it on menus. Today, quinoa is everywhere and in every pantry. That's because it fell into the superfoods category—which is much deserved: it's an amazing protein, high in lysine, mineral rich, high in iron, high in energy, and overall very versatile.

Quinoa is also a problem solver for week night meals, as it cooks quite fast. On a typical day I have to come up with dinner, I want something fast, delicious, and preferably inexpensive. Chicken sausage on sale? That's it! Add mushrooms and quinoa and dinner is done. I prepared this dish one night and my kids raved about it. I used red quinoa, but the golden quinoa is just as good. Even though this is not a stew, this dish reheats very well, so I usually double this recipe. Add a few drops of water to reheat and dinner is ready in no time at all. **Serves 4**

1 cup red quinoa
Kosher salt
5 tablespoons extra-virgin olive oil
1 pound baby bella mushrooms, cleaned and sliced
1 pound chicken sausage (3 or 4 links)
2 cloves garlic, finely minced
1 small onion, chopped
2 scallions, green and white parts, chopped
Freshly ground pepper
Freshly ground nutmeg
Pinch of paprika
2 plum tomatoes, peeled, seeded, and chopped
¼ cup freshly chopped parsley

1. Place the quinoa into a pot and add 2 cups of water and a pinch of salt. Cover the pan, bring to a boil, reduce to a simmer, and cook until it absorbs all the water, about 10 minutes. Stir gently and set aside.

2. Heat a large skillet over medium-high; pour 2 tablespoons of olive oil and swirl the pan around. Add the mushrooms and don't stir for a good 2 minutes, until they start to release their juices. Season lightly with salt and pepper. Stir the mushrooms with a wooden spoon and cook until they just start to soften, about 3 minutes. Transfer the mushrooms to a bowl.

3. Using the same skillet, add the remaining 1 tablespoon olive oil (a little more if you want) and warm the pan over medium heat. Remove the sausage from the case, and add in chunks to the pan, breaking up with a wooden spoon. Cook the sausage all the way through, until it starts to brown, 5 to 7 minutes. Using a slotted spoon, transfer to the bowl with the mushrooms and cover with foil to keep moist.

4. Using the same pan, add the remaining 2 tablespoons olive oil and cook the garlic over low heat until it just starts to turn golden, about 2 minutes. It will cook fast because the pan is already hot.

5. Add the onion, scallions, and season lightly with salt, pepper, nutmeg, and paprika. Stir everything with a wooden spoon, making sure flavors are coming together.

6. Add the tomatoes and continue to cook until they just start to turn mushy, another minute.

7. Pour the mushrooms and chicken sausage into the pan and mix everything together.

8. Add the quinoa and parsley and mix well until blended. Taste and adjust the seasoning. Serve immediately.

Papas y Salsicha Criolla

Sometimes, we have to speak not only for an ingredient, but for a culture that has been undermined, misrepresented, so we reach to the past in search of origin and identity. What our people ate before us can certainly determine who we are and how we eat today.

Here I am, taking a cue from the 70s-era happenings from a Cuban restaurant in Miami, a sub-culture of its own, and creating a recipe that offers flashes of taste and beauty—all the more reason to fall in love with the taste of old food.

This is that kind of dish that is just as easy to cook by instinct as it is to cook by recipe. There is barely any need to measure ingredients. Feel free to use fresh sausage, fully cooked, or semi cured. Depending on the type and consistency of the sausage, you might want to choose to remove the sausage from the case and crumble it up, or to cut into coins and brown the sausage on both sides. The onion mixture is really what gives this dish an amazing flavor. **Serves 4**

3 tablespoons olive oil
6 links (1½ pounds) chicken sausage
4 cloves garlic, minced
4 medium onions, chopped
Kosher salt and freshly ground pepper
Freshly ground nutmeg
1 teaspoon paprika
1 teaspoon ground coriander
2 pounds new potatoes, peeled and cut in half
1 cup water
3 tablespoons freshly chopped parsley

1. In a large saucepan over medium low heat, warm the olive oil. Remove the sausage from the case, and add in chunks to the pan, breaking up with a wooden spoon (or, depending on the type of sausage, you may choose to cut into coins). Cook the sausage all the way through, until it just starts to brown. Using a slotted spoon, transfer to a bowl and cover to keep moist.

2. Using the same pan, add a little bit more oil if necessary, then add the garlic and cook until it just starts to turn golden. Add the onions and cook on very low heat until soft and caramelized, about 30 minutes. Resist the temptation to turn up the heat. You want to cook the onions low and slow, until they caramelize naturally. Season with salt, pepper, nutmeg, paprika, and coriander.

3. Add the potatoes and mix well, allowing them to get hot, stirring occasionally with a wooden spoon, about 5 minutes.

4. Return the sausage to the pan and any accumulated juices left in the bowl and cook with the potato-onion mixture, until all flavors mingle, another 5 minutes.

5. Pour just enough water, about 1 cup, to moisten the whole dish and cover; cook on low and simmer until the potatoes are cooked through and the liquid is very much reduced, about 20 minutes, checking occasionally. You want the onion mixture to enrobe the flavors of the potatoes and sausage in a lovely sauce, but remember this is not a soup; if there is too much liquid after simmering, increase the heat and reduce the sauce a little bit. Finish with parsley and serve hot.

Fish

Grilled Shrimp with Caipirinha Vinaigrette   151

Moroccan Rubbed Red Snapper with Apricot and Hazelnut Sauce   152

Salmon with Pumpkin Sunflower Sauce   155

Salmon Cakes with Coconut Ginger Sauce   157

Spiced Swordfish Skewers   159

Fish with Pepita Sauce   161

Fish Moqueca with Banana, Cashews, and Cilantro   162

Fish with Eggplant and Tomato Sauce   165

Fish Veracruz   167

Sardines with Tomato Olive Salsa   168

Chia-Crusted Salmon with Passion Fruit Sauce   169

Grilled Shrimp with a Caipirinha Vinaigrette

When you're young, you can eat shrimp as much as you want, but since it is high in cholesterol, we should eventually limit our intake, even though it's also high in protein. These days, I count shrimp on the BBQ as a special treat. I prepared this recipe on the Today show during the Rio Olympics in the summer of 2016, when I was rocking the dock at Copacabana beach, cooking, singing, and dancing with tambourines and everyone loved this recipe. It's classic with a modern twist and perfect for a small or large gathering. So, rock with me, cook with me, and dance with me as we prepare this treat! **Serves 4**

½ teaspoon finely grated lime zest

3 tablespoons lime juice

2 tablespoons cachaça

½ teaspoon organic cane sugar

Kosher salt and fresh black pepper

½ cup plus 2 tablespoons extra-virgin olive oil

1 pound medium shrimp (16 to 20), peeled and deveined, tails on

2 tablespoons freshly chopped cilantro

2 tablespoons freshly chopped parsley

1. In a small bowl, whisk together the lime zest, juice, cachaça, sugar, and a small pinch of salt, until the sugar and salt are dissolved.

2. Gradually whisk in ½ cup of the olive oil, a little at a time, until the sauce starts to take on a thicker consistency and is well blended. Sauce can be made up to 3 days ahead of time. Keep it covered in the refrigerator. Bring to room temperature and shake or whisk well before using.

3. In a bowl, season the shrimp with salt, pepper, and the remaining 2 tablespoons of the olive oil. Toss well.

4. Heat a grill on high and oil the grates with cooking spray.

5. Grill the shrimp until just cooked through (opaque in the center) 2 to 3 minutes per side, if that much.

6. Transfer shrimp to a bowl, pour in the vinaigrette, and garnish with cilantro and parsley. Serve on a plate immediately.

Moroccan Rubbed Red Snapper with Apricot and Hazelnut Sauce

I dream of Tangier. The city where my father was born. A unique interpretation of spices and ingredients from around the world, this recipe combines classical cooking with a contemporary touch. It doesn't just taste delicious; this recipe tells a story. It tells my story, of a Latina girl, with a burning passion for health and cooking, looking to find her place in this universe.

Oftentimes, I find myself looking at butter melting in a copper pan, looking for that point where butter becomes golden-nutty, and then I add apricots, hazelnuts, and other herbs and spices. I also find myself quite often preparing rubs. Lots of rubs! I love them; they are easy to prepare, have a long shelf life, and are very unique.

When I cook red snapper with this aromatic spiced Moroccan butter sauce, the incredible aromas that fill the air transport me to Tangier, Morocco, though I've never been there. I always picture the spice markets in Morocco where you can find all the ingredients required for this sauce. In fact, preparing healthy recipes enriched with culture has become one of my favorite projects in the kitchen. **Serves 4**

For the Moroccan Rub:
4 teaspoons kosher salt
1 teaspoon freshly ground black pepper
½ teaspoon ground ginger
½ teaspoon cinnamon
½ teaspoon ground cumin
1 teaspoon smoked paprika
1 teaspoon dried thyme
1 teaspoon dried ground lemon zest

For the Apricot Hazelnut Sauce:
¾ cup (1½ sticks) unsalted butter
3 tablespoons fresh lemon juice
2 tablespoons soy sauce
1 large shallot
1 clove garlic, finely minced
1 teaspoon zaatar
¾ cup diced dried apricots
⅓ cup roughly chopped hazelnuts
3 tablespoons freshly chopped thyme

For the Fish:
4 (5-ounce) red snapper fillets, skin on
3 tablespoons extra-virgin olive oil

1. **Prepare the Rub:** In a small bowl combine all the ingredients. Rub this mixture on both sides of the snapper and let sit at room temperature for 30 minutes. Rub can be prepared up to 1 month ahead of time and kept in a glass container.

2. **Prepare the Sauce:** In a medium saucepan over low heat, melt butter until it develops a light golden-brown color and nutty aroma, about 4 minutes. Add the lemon juice, soy sauce, shallot, and garlic—it will bubble. Cook on low heat, whisking gently for just a minute. Add the zaatar and apricots and swirl the pan around. Remove the pan from the heat and keep aside on the stove.

3. **Prepare the Fish:** Warm 2 tablespoons olive oil in a large skillet. Add the snapper, skin side down, and briefly hold the fillets down with a spatula to prevent the skin from shrinking. Sauté until the bottom of the fillets are lightly dark and crusted, about 5 minutes. Turn and cook until the flesh becomes white and complete opaque, about another 5 minutes.

4. Reheat the sauce gently over low heat and whisk vigorously to blend it smooth. Add the hazelnuts and thyme. To serve, arrange the fish over 4 warm plates, spoon the sauce on top, and serve immediately.

Salmon with Pumpkin Sunflower Sauce

Every recipe has a story. My favorite recipes are those that become my own story and that are so delicious that I have to share with you. This recipe has everything in the punch list: ingredient oriented. Punch. Cooking practicality. Punch. Artistic and delicious results. Punch. Health up. Punch.

You can certainly use a different type of fish, but the flavors of salmon—buttery, slightly smoked fish—combines perfectly with the pumpkin and sunflower seeds. Try to use the center cut of the fish; thin and end pieces cook too fast and do not allow for a rare center. Cook the salmon medium rare, spoon this delicious sauce on top, and see the cook you were born to be! **Serves 4**

8 tablespoons (1 stick) unsalted butter

3 tablespoons fresh lemon juice

2 tablespoons soy sauce

1 shallot, finely minced

Tiny pinch of turbinado sugar

Kosher salt and freshly ground pepper

4 salmon fillets (skinless, about 4–5 ounces each)

1 tablespoon extra-virgin olive oil

⅓ cup pumpkin seeds, roasted

⅓ cup sunflower seeds, lightly roasted

2 tablespoons chopped fresh dill

1. In a medium saucepan over low heat, melt the butter until it develops a nutty aroma and a light golden-brown color. Once the butter starts to turn brown it goes from light to dark quite easily, so keep a close watch. As the butter turns nutty brown, you will see some dark bits on the bottom, and that's fine.

2. Add the lemon juice, soy sauce, shallot, and sugar. Whisk the sauce, then remove the pan from the heat, but keep it in a warm spot on the stove.

3. Season the fish with salt and pepper on both sides. Pour the olive oil into a large nonstick skillet over high heat. Sear the salmon on one side until a golden crust forms, about 4 minutes. Flip the salmon and continue cooking until medium-rare, about 2 more minutes, perhaps a little more depending on the thickness of the fish and desired doneness.

4. Reheat the sauce gently over low heat and whisk vigorously to blend it smooth. Add the pumpkin and sunflower seeds, and dill.

5. To serve, arrange the fish on individual warm plates and spoon the sauce on top.

Salmon Cakes with Coconut Ginger Sauce

Thanks to the power of the Chilean aquaculture, salmon is wildly consumed all over Latin America today. I love this dish because you can make it completely ahead of time and it's great to serve a large crowd. And cooking is fun—I simply can't squeeze any more chopping, sautéing, mixing, stirring, and seasoning into any single dish. Every step of the process is packed full of cooking wonder! This recipe has it all. Serve with wild rice, brown rice, quinoa, or any other grain of your preference. **Serves 4 to 6**

For the Salmon Cakes:

2 slices wheat bread, crust removed
1¼ pounds salmon, skinned and bones removed
1 shallot, minced
1 clove garlic, minced
Zest of 1 lemon
1 tablespoon soy sauce
1 teaspoon sesame oil
¼ cup freshly chopped parsley
¼ cup freshly chopped cilantro
½ teaspoon ground cumin
½ teaspoon Old Bay (tm) seasoning
¼ teaspoon paprika
Kosher salt and freshly ground pepper, to taste
2 eggs
2 tablespoons olive oil

For the Sauce:

2 cloves garlic, minced
1 teaspoon freshly grated ginger
½ onion, finely chopped
4 scallions, green and white parts, chopped
¾ cup fish or shrimp stock (or clam juice)
1 cup coconut milk
½ cup freshly chopped parsley
½ cup freshly chopped cilantro

1. **Prepare the Salmon Cakes:** Place the bread in a food processor and grind to crumbs.

2. Using a very sharp knife, chop the fish very finely (pea-sized pieces) and place in a bowl; add the crumbs, shallot, garlic, lemon zest, soy sauce, sesame oil, herbs and spices, and season lightly with salt and pepper. Mix everything together with your hands (I like using plastic gloves for this task) and finally add the eggs. Shape the mixture into mini patties, about 2 inches in diameter. You should have between 16 to 18 small cakes. Place the cakes in a tray and cover loosely with plastic film; refrigerate the salmon cakes to firm up and develop the flavors, about 15 minutes.

3. **Cook the Salmon Cakes:** Bring a large, deep, 12-inch frying pan to low heat. Warm 2 tablespoons of the olive oil and fry the salmon cakes in batches if necessary, cooking about 2 minutes per side until cakes look nicely caramelized on both sides. Remove the cakes from the pan and place in a tray; cover loosely with foil.

4. **Prepare the Sauce:** Using the same pan, add the remaining 2 tablespoons olive oil and cook the garlic until it just starts to look golden brown—be careful as the pan is already hot from cooking the salmon cakes.

5. Add the ginger and cook for another minute; careful not to burn.

6. Add the onion and scallions and cook, stirring frequently with a wooden spoon, until soft and translucent, another 3 minutes.

(Continued on next page)

7. Add the stock and bring to a boil over high heat.

8. Add the coconut milk and bring back to a boil. Stir everything together, and let the sauce incorporate. Taste and adjust the seasoning with salt and pepper.

9. Lower the heat to the lowest setting and add the salmon cakes, nestling them in the sauce and making sure all of them fit nicely into the pan. If you feel the need to add more liquid, add another 1/4 cup of stock or water, just enough to bring the liquid halfway up the salmon cakes. Cover the pan and simmer gently on low heat for another 5 to 10 minutes, until cake and sauce bond in flavor. Turn off the heat and let the dish rest for another 5 minutes in the pan before serving. Garnish with cilantro and parsley and serve.

6. Add the fish stock and bring to a boil.

7. Add the coconut milk and let it come to a full boil again, then lower the heat to simmer the sauce nice and gently.

8. Remove fish from the oven and carefully transfer fish and all accumulated juices to the sauce. Braise the fish in the sauce over low heat with the pan covered, until the fish is soft and tender, about 5 to 8 minutes.

9. Uncover the pan, add the banana, cashews, and remaining cilantro, and simmer for 4 minutes, enough to bring all flavors together. Divide into plates and spoon plenty of sauce on top. If you'd like a starch on the side, some brown rice would be nice.

Fish with Eggplant and Tomato Sauce

You've probably heard the term nouvelle cuisine *before. Now imagine* Latin nouvelle cuisine. *If you can't imagine, this recipe will take you there. Inspired by chef Claude Troisgros, son of the legendary chef Jean Pierre Troisgros, he landed in Brazil in 1978 after Paul Bocuse asked him if he wanted to spend 2 years in Brazil. Add some 40 years, and he is more Brazilian than ever.*

This dish is very restaurant-style. If it seems too daunting for you, let's consider a few things: you don't need to prepare the green olive oil, just use plain olive oil (although, I do recommend adding some green element to the dish; it can be an herb or even some micro lettuce as garnish). Almost everything can be prepared ahead of time—the tomato sauce can even be frozen. The eggplant can be prepared up to 5 days ahead and reheated before serving. The fish, of course, you want to buy fresh and cook just before serving. Trust me on this, you want to make this recipe—it works, it feeds, it nourishes and works again; a celebration of the explosive power of cooking. **Serves 4**

For the Green Olive Oil:
1 bunch watercress, leaves and
     upper stems
$\frac{1}{3}$ cup olive oil

For the Tomato Sauce:
2 tablespoons extra-virgin
     olive oil
1 clove garlic, roughly chopped
1 large onion, roughly chopped
8 plum tomatoes, peeled,
     seeded, and roughly
     chopped
$\frac{1}{2}$ cup water
Kosher salt and freshly ground
     black pepper
Freshly grounded nutmeg

For the Eggplant:
$1\frac{1}{3}$ cups balsamic vinegar
$\frac{1}{2}$ cup + 2 tablespoons honey
2 tablespoons extra-virgin
     olive oil
2 globe eggplants, sliced into
     rounds (about $\frac{1}{4}$-inch thick)

1. **Prepare the Green Olive Oil:** place the olive oil and watercress in a blender, and buzz on high speed until smooth, about 3 minutes. Strain and reserve.

2. **Prepare the Tomato Sauce**: In a medium saucepan warm the olive oil over low heat and add the garlic; cook until it just begins to turn golden. Add the onion and cook until soft, about 2 minutes. Add the tomatoes and cook, stirring frequently until it begins to soften, another 2 minutes. Add the water and bring to a boil; season with salt and pepper and nutmeg, reduce the heat to low, and cook until it's nice and tasty, about 10 minutes. Puree in a blender until completely smooth. You don't need to strain this sauce. Just pour back into the pan and reserve. Sauce can be prepared up to 3 days ahead of time and kept in a covered plastic container in the fridge.

3. **Prepare the Eggplant**: In a medium saucepan, pour the balsamic vinegar and honey and bring to a boil. Reduce the heat to medium and cook until the consistency becomes syrupy, about 5 minutes. Reserve. You can prepare this balsamic reduction up to 3 days ahead of time and keep it covered in the fridge.

4. Season eggplant slices with salt and pepper on both sides.

(Continued on next page)

For the Fish:

4 (6-ounce) red snapper fillets

¼ cup all-purpose
   (or Wondra) flour

2 tablespoons extra-virgin
   olive oil

2 springs parsley or rosemary,
   to garnish
   (or any other herb)

5. Working in batches, in a large nonstick sauté pan, warm the olive oil and cook eggplant on both sides until nice and golden, about 3 minutes per side. Remove the eggplant to a plate and repeat with all slices. When all eggplant is done, return a few slices to the pan at very high heat, enough to make one layer covering the pan, add about ¼ cup of the balsamic reduction, and brown the eggplant on both sides, about 1 minute per side. Repeat the process with all eggplant slices, always working in batches. Warning: A lot of smoke will come up when you add the balsamic reduction. It's okay. Don't let the vinegar mixture reduce completely. You want the eggplant to still be moist. Set aside.

6. **Prepare the Fish:** Make 3 or 4 light incisions on the skin-side of the fish. Season the snapper with salt and pepper on both sides and dust lightly with flour, shaking off the excess. In a large nonstick skillet, warm the olive oil over medium heat. Add the fish to the skillet, skin side down, and briefly hold the fillets down with a spatula to prevent the skin from shrinking. Cook until the bottom of the fillets are golden and crusted, about 5 minutes. Turn and cook for about 5 minutes longer, until the flesh is completely opaque.

7. **Assemble the dish:** Use a ladle to pour some of the tomato sauce on the bottom of each plate and spread into a circle. Arrange 3 to 4 eggplant slices on top and place a fillet in each center. Drizzle a little bit of the green olive oil all around and garnish with a sprig of parsley or rosemary.

Fish Veracruz

If there is one dish I grew up on that represents the pinnacle of healthy home cooking in my teen years, it's Fish Veracruz, originated in that state in Mexico. Except that in Rio, we didn't call that, we called it simply Peixe com Molho de Cebola e Tomate, *which is exactly what this recipe is (fish braised in onion and tomatoes). Today, I like to jazz it up a little by adding capers, dill, and lemon zest. I used to eat this dish with whatever fish the vendors convinced my mother to buy. And you can do the same, because this dish is really very flexible; it can be prepared with tilapia, red snapper, halibut, monkfish, or cod, which I am using here. Feel free to use canned tomatoes already peeled if you'd like.* **Serves 4**

Zest of 1 lemon
3 cloves garlic, minced
4 (6-ounce) skinless cod fillets, about 1–1½-inch thick
3 tablespoons extra-virgin olive oil
1 onion, sliced thin
Kosher salt
Freshly ground black pepper
1 teaspoon dried oregano
¼ teaspoon paprika
4 plum tomatoes, peeled, seeded, and sliced
¼ cup white wine
¾ cup chicken stock
1 tablespoon capers, drained
2 tablespoons fresh dill, chopped

1. **Marinate the Fish:** Using the flat part of a chef's knife, mash together the lemon zest with 1 clove garlic. Rub that on both sides of the fish, place them on a plate, pour 1 tablespoon olive oil over, and cover with plastic wrap. Let it marinate for 15 minutes while you prepare the sauce.

2. **Prepare the Sauce:** On a large skillet, warm the remaining 2 tablespoons of olive oil on low heat and add the remaining 2 garlic cloves, cooking until just lightly golden brown.

3. Add the onion and cook, stirring occasionally with a wooden spoon until soft and translucent, about 5 minutes. Season lightly with salt and pepper.

4. Add the oregano and paprika and toast the spices in the onion.

5. Add the tomatoes, and cook, stirring occasionally, until it just starts to soften, about 3 minutes.

6. Add the wine and let it cook down and evaporate.

7. Add the chicken stock and let it come to a boil, then lower heat again.

8. Season fish with salt and pepper on both sides. Add the fish to the pot, carefully placing in the sauce and spooning over the top. Cover the pan and cook gently, until the fish just starts to flake apart, between 8 to 10 minutes depending on the heat.

9. Taste the broth and adjust the seasoning. Finish by adding capers and dill all over.

10. Transfer to individual plates and spoon sauce over each piece of fish.

Sardines with Tomato Olive Salsa

The word "sardine" comes from the word "Sardenha," which is an island of the coast of Italy, where the fish is abundant. You will also find sardines all over the coast in Brazil and South America.

An incredibly healthy fish, sardines are full of omega-3 fatty acids and have a unique taste. This recipe is not to be underestimated by its simplicity. Magic in the world of food often relies on simple and fresh ingredients that you might have; this tomato-olive salsa complements the umami taste of sardines.

Serves 4

For the Tomato Olive Salsa:

½ pound cherry tomatoes, halved

⅓ cup kalamata olives, pitted and halved

1 tablespoon finely minced red onion

¼ cup fresh chopped parsley

¼ cup fresh chopped chives

¼ cup extra-virgin olive oil, plus 4 tablespoons for sardines

Kosher salt and freshly ground pepper

For the Sardines:

Kosher salt and freshly ground black pepper

1½ pounds fresh sardines (8 to 12 large), filleted, bones removed

½ cup Wondra flour

2 tablespoons olive oil

1. **Make the Salsa:** In a large bowl combine the cherry tomatoes, olives, and red onion. Mix in the herbs and toss well. Drizzle the olive oil and combine everything. Season to taste with salt and pepper. Set aside.

2. **Cook the Sardines:** Season the sardine fillets with salt and pepper on both sides. Dust with Wondra flour on both sides and shake off the excess. Pour the olive oil over a large skillet at medium-high heat. Add the sardines in a single layer. Cook, lightly pressing the sardines flat with a spatula as they curl, just until golden brown, about 1 minute. Flip them and cook them on the other side, for another minute. Be careful not to overcook them. Transfer them to a platter. Arrange the tomato olive salsa on top and serve warm.

Chia-Crusted Salmon with Passion Fruit Sauce

For the many years I've cooked in professional kitchens, I still love to prepare meals that not only taste like restaurant-style but look it as well. And there is no one I love to serve these more than to my kids. I really feel that bringing them up "on food" is an education in itself. Our dinner conversations range from the impact of social media on our lives, to politics, to cultural differences between Latin America and the US. And at almost every dinner, we talk about food and restaurants.

This recipe could cost up to $30 in a nice fancy New York–style restaurant! The distinguished taste of salmon pairs perfectly with the tangy passion fruit in this buttery sauce. Another layer of awesomeness is the chia seed crust. It works wonders! **Serves 4**

For the Passion Fruit Sauce:
4 tablespoons unsalted butter
1 tablespoon vegetable oil
½ cup passion fruit pulp
⅛ teaspoon organic cane sugar
1 teaspoon white wine vinegar
1 tablespoon minced shallot (about half a shallot)
½ teaspoon mustard
Kosher salt and freshly ground pepper
2 tablespoons freshly chopped cilantro

For the Fish:
¾ cup chia seeds
4 (6-ounce) salmon fillets, skin-on
3 tablespoons extra-virgin olive oil

Prepare the Sauce:
1. In a small saucepan, melt the butter over low heat until lightly brown and nutty, about 4 minutes. Add the vegetable oil and whisk well. Pour into a glass measuring cup and keep warm at the back of the stove.

2. In another small saucepan, place the passion pulp, sugar, vinegar, and shallot, and simmer gently over low heat, stirring often, until reduced by about half (to about ¼ cup). Transfer to a bowl and cool to room temperature.

3. Add the mustard to the passion fruit and mix well.

4. Little by little, whisk the melted butter into the passion fruit reduction until it forms a creamy consistency. Season lightly with salt and pepper. Reserve.

Prepare the Fish:
1. Place the chia seeds on a large plate. Season the salmon with salt and pepper on both sides, then turn and press the top side down directly onto the chia seeds, applying pressure to make sure the seeds stick.

2. Heat a large nonstick skillet over high heat. Add the olive oil and swirl the pan around. Cook the salmon seed side down until you see the color of the fish starting to change on the sides, about 3 minutes; carefully flip and cook on the other side for just another minute for medium rare. If you like your salmon a little more well done, cook a little longer.

3. Transfer the fish to a plate and spoon the sauce over. Garnish with cilantro and serve.

Side Dishes and Bowls

Feijao Tropeiro   172

Jeweled Carrot Rice   174

Baião de Dois   175

Rice and Beans the Modern Way   177

Whole Wheat Fusilli with Chicken and Avocado Cashew Pesto   178

Quinoa Risotto with Peas and Turkey Bacon   181

Yucca Latkes   183

Farofa   185

Butternut Mash with Arugula Pesto   187

Flaxseed-Crusted Tamale Cakes   188

Black Bean Burger   190

Broccoli Fajitas with Cashew-Peanut Vinaigrette   192

Tacos Pico de Gallo   195

Mexican Creamed Corn   197

Ricotta-Stuffed Zucchini   198

Feijao Tropeiro

This recipes translates to "Beans with Sausage, Kale, and Manioc Starch." I can't count the number of ways to eat a bowl of beans: sometimes in a soup, in a rice dish, in a stew, with kale, with sausage, and sometimes, just plain beans. This recipe is inspired by a classic dish in Brazil called Feijão Tropeiro. The word tropeiro refers to cowboys and rangers who traveled great distances in search of suitable territory for raising cattle and relied mostly on canned food to carry with them on long expeditions: beans, meat (mostly jerky), and manioc flour. I make it with chicken sausage. You can certainly use canned beans, though as a Brazilian, I remain faithful to cooking my beans in my pressure cooker. **Serves 4**

Kosher salt and freshly ground black pepper

16 ounces kale

2 tablespoons extra-virgin olive oil

3 chicken sausage links (about ½ pounds), sliced into ¼-thick slices

3 cloves garlic, finely minced

1 onion, finely chopped (about 1 cup)

2 scallions (white and green parts), chopped, plus more for garnish

Freshly ground nutmeg

3 cups cooked red kidney beans

1 tablespoon unsalted butter

¼ cup manioc flour (*farinha de mandioca)*

tablespoons fresh parsley

1. Bring a pot of water to a boil and add a pinch of salt. Plunge the kale leaves into boiling water, and cook until it's just tender, 2 to 3 minutes. Using a slotted spoon, remove blanched kale from the water, letting most of the water drip on to a bowl. Let it cool then chop roughly.

2. In a large 12-inch pan, warm the olive oil over medium-low heat. Add the sausage and cook until it just starts to brown and crisp, about 5 minutes. Using a slotted spoon, transfer to a bowl and cover with foil to keep moist. If there is too much rendered fat, spoon some out.

3. Using the same pan, add the garlic and cook until it just starts to turn lightly golden brown, about 2 minutes.

4. Add the onion and scallions, and cook until soft, mixing often with a wooden spoon, about 5 minutes. Season with salt, pepper, and nutmeg.

5. Add the cooked beans, sausage, and kale, and mix well. Taste and adjust the seasoning. You can prepare the recipe up to this point and keep it in the back of the stove, or chill in a plastic container for up to 5 days.

6. In a medium saucepan, melt the butter over medium-low heat. Add the manioc flour and stir constantly with a wooden spoon, toasting the flour until it reaches a light golden color. Transfer the mixture to a bowl and season with salt and pepper.

7. Just before serving, sprinkle the flour-butter mixture over the beans; don't dump it all at once. Instead, sprinkle a little at a time, and keep mixing with a wooden spoon. The flour absorbs a lot of moisture, so use your judgment. I like to add a little bit to the mixture and serve a little on the side of the bowl. Garnish with parsley and scallions and serve warm.

Jeweled Carrot Rice

This recipe is inspired by the jeweled rice that I often eat my aunt Sarita's. She is a Jewish immigrant originally from Morocco, who came to Rio de Janeiro in the 1960s and adapted to the new tropical land, while keeping her roots and faith intact. She prepares a variety of jeweled rice dishes. The carrots add a natural sweetness to the rice and makes it the perfect side dish for a healthy meal. **Serves 6 to 8**

2 cups brown basmati rice

2 tablespoons olive oil

Half an onion, finely diced

2½ teaspoons kosher salt

2 cups grated carrots (about 4 medium carrots, grated on the smallest hole)

Pinch saffron thread

3⅓ cups water

½ cup sliced almonds, lightly toasted

½ cup chopped pitted Picholine olives

¼ cup chopped parsley

1. Rinse the rice in cold water several times to remove the excess starch. On the final wash, drain the rice in a colander and let it sit for 5 minutes to dry.

2. On a medium saucepan over low heat, add the olive oil and cook the onion until soft, about 3 minutes.

3. Add the rice, salt, carrots, and saffron, and mix them with a wooden spoon until the grains are warm and coated with oil.

4. Pour in the cold water, cover partway, and cook the rice over medium heat until it's soft and tender, about 20 minutes.

5. Fluff the rice and stir in the almonds, olives, and parsley. Transfer to a bowl and serve hot.

Baião de Dois

Stir fry Brazilian style! Singer and songwriter Luiz Gonzaga, known in Brazil as Gonzaguinha, was not only crazy about music but also about the cuisine of his native state of Pernanbuco. One of his favorite dishes was Baião de Dois and he sang plenty about it in the lyrics of his songs, which most likely fall into a category of Brazilian music called Forró.

In the northeast, dishes taste of coconut, cashews, ginger, cilantro, lime, and peppers. In this dish, rice and beans are cooked together, and while the food may look Brazilian, it has its own distinct flavor: fresh and smoky, and predicated on the balance of rice and beans. You may skip a few items, but the fact that Baião de Dois has made the transition from the east corners of Brazil to my American kitchen, is totally entertaining. And I am sure you will be entertained as well! **Serves 10**

8 cups chicken stock
2 tablespoons olive oil
5 cloves garlic, minced
2 pounds brown rice, such as
    jasmine or basmati
3 bay leaves
1 teaspoon paprika
Kosher salt
¼ pound turkey bacon, diced
¼ pound chicken sausage,
    diced or crumbled
1 red onion, diced
1 green bell pepper, diced
2 plum tomatoes, peeled,
    seeded, and diced
1 pound black eyed peas,
    cooked and drained
½ pound cooked and pulled
    chicken meat (from one
    chicken breast)
¼ cup fresh chopped cilantro
1 scallion, white and green
    parts, chopped
¼ pound feta cheese, cut
    into ¼-inch cubes (or
    queso-blanco)
Freshly ground black pepper

1. Bring the chicken stock to a simmer over low heat on the back of the stove.

2. In a large saucepan over medium heat, warm the olive oil; add the garlic and cook until it just begins to turn golden.

3. Add the rice, bay leaves, and paprika; reduce the heat to low, season with salt, and stir well with a wooden spoon, until rice is shiny and each grain is covered with oil.

4. Pour in chicken stock, stir to distribute liquid evenly, then cover the pan. Cook until rice is just cooked, about 15 minutes.

5. Meanwhile in another large skillet, over medium-high heat, add the turkey bacon and chicken sausage and cook in its own fat (add a little more olive oil if necessary) until it just starts to get crispy, about 4 minutes.

6. Reduce heat to low, add the onion and green bell pepper, and cook, stirring frequently with a wooden spoon, until it gets soft and tender, another 4 minutes.

7. Add the tomatoes and cook until they start to get mushy and release water, about 3 minutes.

8. Add the cooked beans and pulled chicken and stir well. Season with salt and pepper.

9. Add the cooked rice and stir everything together.

10. Garnish with cilantro, scallion, and cheese on top. Sprinkle fresh pepper and serve hot.

Rice and Beans the Modern Way

What can be more classic in Latin food than rice and beans? Well, while many will argue that there is something quite healthy about it, I am trying to make this dish even more healthy and fun, with a bit of inspiration from superfoods and keeping total health in mind. As a Latina, I grew up on rice and beans, but after I developed this recipe, I have been serving this version ever since. Trust me, you will like this. You will really like this! **Serves 6 to 8**

1 cup wild rice
1 cup brown basmati rice
4 tablespoons canola oil, divided
Kosher salt
2 cloves garlic, finely minced
½ green bell pepper, finely diced
1 teaspoon ground cumin
2 cups cooked and drained black beans
¼ cup fresh chopped parsley
¼ cup fresh chopped cilantro
¼ cup fresh chopped dill
Freshly ground black pepper
1 cup crispy kale

1. Place the wild rice in a medium pan and cover with water, at least 2 inches above the rice level. Cover the pan and simmer on low heat until the rice is tender, about 45 minutes. Drain and set aside.

2. Wash the brown rice in cold water. Drain in a colander and air dry for 5 minutes. Warm 2 tablespoons of the canola oil in a medium saucepan over low heat, add the rice and stir with a wooden spoon, making sure all the grains are covered in oil and shining bright. Add 3 cups of water, 2 teaspoons kosher salt, and partially cover the pan. Bring to a boil, then reduce the heat to low until the rice is tender, about 15 minutes.

3. In another saucepan, warm the remaining 2 tablespoons canola oil over medium heat and cook the garlic until it just starts to turn golden, about 2 minutes.

4. Add the green bell pepper and cook, stirring frequently with a wooden spoon until it starts to soften, about 5 minutes.

5. Season with salt, pepper, and cumin, and cook stirring everything together.

6. Add the black beans and cook for another minute or two, just for the beans to take flavor. Transfer to a large bowl.

7. Add the wild rice and basmati rice to the beans. Add the herbs. Taste and adjust the seasoning if necessary. Just before serving, add the crispy kale. Serve warm or at room temperature.

Whole Wheat Fusilli with Chicken and Avocado Cashew Pesto

It's a joy to have a favorite food at a favorite restaurant. In fact, I have many of them. One of them is this Pasta with Avocado Cashew Pesto that I ate at By Chole, a vegan restaurant in New York City. I keep going back over and over, not only because it's healthy, but because it's so delicious. This dish is served at the restaurant without any protein; at home, I added chicken to feed my two hungry foodie-teenagers. **Serves 4**

For the Avocado Cashew Pesto:

Makes 3 cups

1 cup cashews, unsalted, lightly toasted
1 small clove garlic
1 cup packed fresh cilantro leaves
1 cup packed fresh parsley leaves
2 avocados
2 tablespoons lemon juice
Kosher salt and freshly ground pepper
½ cup extra-virgin olive oil

1 pound skinless chicken breast tenderloins
Kosher salt and freshly ground pepper
2 tablespoons extra-virgin olive oil
1 clove garlic, minced
1 shallot, minced
1 pound whole wheat fusilli
6–8 tablespoons avocado pesto

1. **Make the Pesto:** Place the nuts, garlic, cilantro, and parsley in a food processor; pulse to combine.

2. Peel and pit the avocados, and add them to the food processor, along with 2 tablespoons lemon juice. Season lightly with salt and pepper. Pulse until blended. With the machine running, pour the remaining olive oil in a steady stream to create an emulsion. Taste and adjust the seasoning.

3. Pesto can be done up to 5 days ahead of time. Reserve in a container covered with a tight-fitting lid in the refrigerator.

4. **Cook the Chicken:** Cut the chicken into small pieces of about 1 inch and season with salt and pepper.

5. In a large pan, warm the olive oil and add the garlic; cook until it just starts to turn golden, about 2 minutes. Add the shallot and cook, stirring occasionally with a wooden spoon. Add the chicken pieces, and cook, stirring occasionally with a wooden spoon until the chicken is lightly golden and just cooked, about 5 minutes. Remove from the heat and cover the pan.

6. **Cook the Pasta:** Bring a large pot of water to a boil over high heat and add a good pinch of salt. Cook the pasta al dente according the package instructions. Save some cooking liquid just in case. Drain well and transfer to a bowl.

7. Add the pasta to the chicken and mix well, heating all the way through. You may want to add some of the pasta water.

8. When you are ready to serve, add the avocado cashew pesto and mix well, making sure every piece of chicken and every piece of pasta is well coated with pesto. Taste and adjust the seasoning; if it needs a bit more liquid, add some more reserved pasta water. Serve immediately.

Quinoa Risotto with Peas and Turkey Bacon

You love risotto—welcome to the club! Risotto is very popular in Latin America due to the large number of Italian immigrants in the region. The south of Brazil, for example, has a huge Italian influence. I have always been a huge fan of a classic Italian risotto, but when I tried this combination, it was an aha moment. This recipe will not disappoint you, and you can take quinoa in so many different directions. There are, however, a couple things to consider: quinoa will not expand the way Arborio rice does, so if you need to feed more than 4 people, by all means double the recipe. Also, quinoa cooks a bit faster than rice, so dinner will be ready sooner!

Like any risotto, we are talking about a blank canvas recipe. Peas and smoked meat go very well, so I use this concept here. Next time, you may wish to try it with other ingredients. That's the beauty of risotto.

Serves 2 to 4

3¼ cups chicken stock
2 tablespoons olive oil
2 tablespoon unsalted butter
1 medium onion, chopped
4 strips (110g) turkey bacon, roughly chopped
1¼ cups (200 g) quinoa
½ cup dry white wine
Kosher salt and freshly ground pepper
Freshly ground nutmeg
1 cup (140g) peas
¼ cup freshly chopped parsley
¼ freshly grated Parmesan cheese

1. In a medium saucepan, bring the stock to a simmer.

2. In another large, heavy saucepan, melt 1 tablespoon of the butter and 2 tablespoons olive oil. Add the onion and turkey bacon and cook, stirring frequently, until soft and slightly golden, about 4 minutes.

3. Add the quinoa and stir frequently, until the grains are warm, shiny, and coated with the onion mixture, about 3 minutes.

4. Add the wine and bring to a boil until the liquid is almost all absorbed, about 2 minutes.

5. Slowly add one ladle of hot stock and allow the quinoa to cook, stirring often, until the liquid is absorbed. Adjust the heat to maintain a gentle simmer. Add another ladle and repeat the process. Continue adding ladles of stock only when the previous addition has been completely absorbed. Cook until the quinoa is tender but still firm to the bite, about 15 minutes. Season lightly with salt and pepper and nutmeg.

6. Don't let the risotto get too thick: you are looking for a creamy consistency, just as if you were using Arborio rice. The quinoa will absorb all 3 cups of liquid. Add the peas, parsley, and Parmesan, then taste the dish, checking for flavor and doneness. Just before serving, add the remaining ¼ cup stock and remaining tablespoon butter. Serve immediately.

Yucca Latkes

The Jewish community in Latin America is tiny. Argentina leads the way, and then comes Brazil, which happens to be the second largest Catholic country in the world. I was raised Jewish in Rio (Hello Shabbat, hello bikini!) where parties and celebrations are a constant way of living. At Christmas dinner, when the whole country is celebrating the biggest holiday, I would get together with my Jewish friends and we would celebrate it our way, with Turkey and Farofa. For Hanukka, we eat latkes and sufganiot (little fried doughnuts).

You know me—since immigrating to America, I always like to add my Latin touch to festivities and I'm always coming up with new ideas and fusions between Brazilian and American cuisines, like this recipe for Yucca Latkes. While the vegetable is quite firm when raw, once cooked, it becomes this creamy, supple vegetable, and in this latke format it gets super crunchy on the outside.

This recipe is not very big, and the yucca latkes are on the small size, so if you have a crowd to feed, double the recipe. Pay attention to the yucca: unlike the yucca sold in Latin America, close to the source, yucca travels far to hit the American grocery stores. The good news is that in this era of global cooking and online shopping, you can find yucca at most regular stores. Whenever I buy yucca in New England, I tend to buy a few more, because sometimes the yucca appears to be okay but on the inside they're a little old or have brown spots. You want yucca that is firm, plain white on the inside, and releasing a starchy drop when cut open. Yucca has a woody fiber in the center, and the older the yucca gets, the tougher this fiber is. Be sure to remove it. **Makes 12 small pancakes**

2 medium yuccas, about
   1½ pounds total
2 egg whites
2 tablespoons grated Parmesan
Kosher salt and freshly ground
   black pepper
Freshly grated nutmeg
3 tablespoons unsalted butter
⅓ cup canola oil

1. Peel both the outer brown layer and the inner white layer of the yucca. Wash the yucca and cut in half, and then in quarters lengthwise. Remove the woody center if the yucca has one (most do). Use a food processor to grate the yucca (or grate by hand) and turn into a bowl (you should have about 2 cups).

2. Add the egg whites, Parmesan, and season well with salt, pepper, and nutmeg. Mix well, making sure yucca is nicely coated and well-seasoned.

3. Heat butter and oil in a large shallow frying pan over medium heat. Scoop about 2 tablespoons of the yucca mixture and use your hands to press into small, thin patties. Working in batches, place them in the pan, without adding too many at once. Fry them over medium heat until golden, about 2 minutes on each side. Remove from the oil and place on a sheet pan lined with paper towels while you cook the rest. Serve hot as a side dish or main course. You can reheat these latkes quite easily in a 350°F oven for 10 minutes.

Farofa

If you want to lose your veganity in Rio, I've got the place for you: Teva. Spinning a new vegan tale in Rio de Janeiro ain't an easy job, but that's exactly what Chef Daniel Biron did when he opened Teva. It not only has a vegan menu, but Daniel also takes a lesson from nature: natural recycled wood, minimal food waste, locally sourced food, and a friendly social environment all around. It's a labor of love. Every detail comes from a true thing—something he's learned, something he's seen, something he knows.

Farofa is a side dish made from Farinha de mandioca, or manioc flour. Manioc is an iconic root vegetable in Latin cooking; you may also find it under names such as yucca or cassava. Farofa is a dish reminiscent of the native Indians, who did not include much flamboyance or embellishment in their cuisine. Most Brazilians love to eat plain and simple farofa as a side dish, or as a complement to rice and beans, adding a nutty and crunchy element to the soft combo—the way bread crumbs are added to mac and cheese.

Daniel does it differently, adding lots of ingredients to this farofa, and keeping it interesting bite after bite. First, he makes a magical mixture of toasted garlic and Brazil nuts, then he adds leeks, onions, banana, raisins, and scallions. Who needs anything else? Or, you could add a fried egg on top, and call it a dinner.

Serves 2 to 4

5 tablespoons extra-virgin olive oil

1 cup manioc flour

Kosher salt and freshly ground black pepper

4 cloves garlic, minced

¼ cup Brazil nuts, roughly chopped

1 small leek, chopped

Half onion, finely chopped

¼ teaspoon turmeric

1 banana, sliced into coins

¼ cup dark raisins, soaked in warm water

2 scallions, white and green parts, sliced thin on a bias

¼ cup fresh parsley, roughly chopped

¼ cup fresh cilantro, roughly chopped

1. In a small pan, pour 2 tablespoons of the olive oil and add the manioc flour to toast on low heat. Watch it closely or else the flour will burn. Keep cooking until the flour toasts to a light golden color, about 3 minutes. Season lightly with salt and pepper. Transfer flour to a plate and wipe the pan to use again for the onion.

2. In another skillet, over low heat, pour 1 tablespoon of olive oil and cook the garlic, until it just starts to turn lightly golden, about 1 minute. Add the Brazil nuts and continue to cook until lightly toasted and fragrant, about 2 minutes more. Turn off the heat and set aside.

3. Using the pan of the toasted flour, pour the remaining 2 tablespoons olive oil and cook the leek and onion on low heat, until soft and translucent, about 5 minutes. Add the toasted flour, the garlic/nut mixture, turmeric, banana slices (being careful not to mash them), raisins, and a pinch of the scallions, parsley, and cilantro, and combine. Spoon onto a nice plate and garnish with the remaining scallions, parsley, and cilantro.

burgers and cook until the outside is crisp and lightly browned, turning once, about 3 minutes per side. Remove from the pan.

6.   Using the same pan, sear the buns to suck up all the brown bits; place the burger in the buns, with lettuce, tomato, and red onion. Serve immediately.

Broccoli Fajitas with Cashew-Peanut Vinaigrette

Do you really want to know the secret to eating vegetables? You have to make interesting things with it. Serve plain steamed broccoli to anyone and see how excited they'll be to eat it. No wonder why plain broccoli is the symbol of a tasteless diet. Especially for people living with type 2 diabetes, this is the kind of diet they fear they'll have to eat for the rest of their lives! But as the spokesperson of a healthy living campaign, I'm always coming up with interesting recipes, and you don't have to sacrifice flavor to eat a healthy and delicious meal! The proof is in the broccoli. Warm some nice tortillas, spread a spicy orange sauce on the bottom, roast some broccoli, and top it with a cashew-peanut vinaigrette. Now that's a reason to get excited to eat this Broccoli Fajita! Who knew broccoli could taste so good? **Serves 4 to 6**

For the Broccoli:
1 pound broccoli, stems peeled and
    cut into long spears
2 tablespoons olive oil
Kosher salt and freshly ground black
    pepper

For the Cashew-Peanut Vinaigrette:
¼ cup raw unsalted cashews, roughly
    chopped
¼ cup raw unsalted peanuts, roughly
    chopped
7 tablespoons extra-virgin olive oil,
    divided
1 teaspoon kosher salt
2 teaspoons fresh lime juice

For the Spicy Orange Salsa:
2 tablespoons orange marmalade
1 teaspoon orange zest (more for garnish)
2 tablespoons Dijon mustard
1 teaspoon aji amarillo paste
2 tablespoons low-fat mayonnaise
4–6 whole wheat tortillas
2 tablespoons freshly chopped cilantro
6–8 orange wedges (from the zested
    orange)

1. **Prepare the Broccoli:** Preheat the oven to 375°F. Toss the broccoli in a bowl with olive oil, salt, and pepper. Spread on a large baking sheet and roast until cooked and crunchy, flipping once halfway through roasting time, about 20 minutes total.

2. **Prepare the Cashew-Peanut Vinaigrette:** In a small saucepan, combine the nuts, 1 tablespoon of the olive oil, and salt, and cook, stirring constantly (don't go anywhere!) over medium heat until the nuts are toasted, about 5 minutes. Transfer to a plate and let them cool completely.

3. Place the lime juice in a bowl. Add the remaining olive oil in a steady stream, whisking constantly to create an emulsion. Season lightly with salt and pepper, then add the nuts and any accumulated juices from the plate. Add the cilantro.

4. **Prepare the Spicy Orange Salsa:** In a bowl, mix all the ingredients together.

5. **Assemble:** To serve, heat a medium skillet over medium heat. Working one at a time, cook the tortillas just until warmed through, then transfer to plates. Spread the tortillas with Spicy Orange Salsa, and arrange some broccoli over. Top with the Cashew-Peanut Vinaigrette and cilantro. Sprinkle some orange zest and serve with orange wedges.

Tacos Pico de Gallo

Pico de Gallo *is a very simple raw salsa, also called* salsa fresca, *made with tomatoes, serrano chiles, cilantro, and onions. Traditionally, pico de gallo is made with chopped tomatoes, producing tons of yummy juices, and is served in many Latin restaurants with tortillas, almost like a bread basket, as soon as you sit down. I wanted to take this idea and apply to a healthy dinner concept, one that you can assemble in under 10 minutes. Instead of chopping the tomatoes and making the pico de gallo in a juicy sauce, I take the same ingredients and assemble in a warm multigrain tortilla.*

This is simple and healthy food at its fastest! With good and fresh ingredients, a taco as simple as this can be exquisite, even if it's assembled in 10 minutes and gone in 3 bites. And that's the whole point! While in Mexico we eat tacos as a snack, in my American kitchen, tacos make a lovely lunch or dinner.

Use this recipe as your blank canvas for Latin food. You can add avocados, radishes, scallions, grilled or shredded chicken, or anything else you want. The choice of tortilla makes a huge difference in your taco. Corn and flour tortillas are the most common. I like to use multigrain to stay on the healthy side, but feel free to choose your tortillas. It's important that they're served warm, and never reheated, as the starch doesn't react well when it's cooled and warmed up again. **Makes 4 tacos**

8 vine tomatoes

Kosher salt and freshly ground pepper

8 multigrain, wheat flour tortillas

½ red onion, thinly sliced

¼ cup freshly chopped cilantro

2 serrano chiles, thinly sliced

2 tablespoons olive oil

2 limes, cut into wedges

1. Prepare the filling: Cut the tomatoes in half and then into slices. Season with salt and pepper.

2. Heat a medium skillet over medium heat. Working one at a time, cook the tortillas just until warmed through, and transfer to plates. Spread the tomatoes, red onion, chopped cilantro, and serrano chiles on the tacos. Drizzle a little bit of olive oil over. Squeeze a couple of lime wedges over the filling. Fold the tacos in half, two per plate, and serve with more lime wedges. Don't worry if the tacos don't stay folded. You can grab them with your hands anyway and fold to eat.

Mexican Creamed Corn

Yellow and green, the colors of Brazil serve as a metaphor for this very Mexican dish, incredibly delicious and so easy to prepare. "Sin mais, no hay pais"—without corn, there is no country. It's a classic saying in Mexico. Indeed, it's hard to imagine the whole cooking of Latin America without corn. As a Latin-American chef, I feel blessed to live in a country where corn is such a staple. This dish is the perfect blend of Mexican traditions using one of the most prized ingredients in both countries: corn. It's pure, simple, healthy, and easy. In Mexico, this recipe calls for a bit of a kick, either with jalapeno, habanero, poblano, or serrano. For my kids, I like to use a small piece of jalapeno and green bell pepper. A note to remember: be careful when handling jalapenos, habaneros, or other chiles; the capsaicin (responsible for the heat) sticks to the skin even after washing your hands, so I recommend using gloves, and avoid rubbing your face after handling chiles. **Serves 4**

2 tablespoons olive oil
½ jalapeno, ribs and seeds removed, finely chopped
½ green bell pepper, chopped
1 shallot, finely chopped
4 ears corn, kernels scraped
1 cup water
½ cup plain low-fat yogurt
Kosher salt and freshly ground black pepper
¼ cup crumbled feta cheese or *queso-blanco*
3 tablespoons freshly chopped cilantro

1. In a medium saucepan, heat the olive oil over medium heat. Cook the jalapeno, green bell pepper, and shallot, stirring with a wooden spoon, until soft, about 4 minutes.

2. Add the corn kernels and water. Cook, stirring frequently, until corn is tender, 5 to 7 minutes.

3. Remove from the heat, add the yogurt, and season with salt and pepper. Garnish with feta cheese and cilantro. Serve immediately.

Ricotta-Stuffed Zucchini

Zucchini and ricotta: it's a combination that oozes freshness and satisfaction. When eaten, this duo of hues evokes the progression of a perfect vegetarian dinner, each bite more delicious than the previous one. Accent with light Parmesan cheese and make your dinner really glow. **Serves 4**

4 medium zucchinis, cut in half
    lengthwise
6 tablespoons olive oil
3 cloves garlic, finely minced
2 shallots, finely chopped
2 tablespoons dried oregano
Freshly grated nutmeg
$1/4$ teaspoon paprika
2 plum tomatoes, peeled,
    seeded, and chopped
2 cups fresh ricotta cheese
$3/4$ cup freshly grated
    Parmesan
$3/4$ cup whole wheat bread
    crumbs
$1/4$ cup freshly chopped parsley
2 egg yolks
Kosher salt and freshly ground
    pepper

1. Scoop out the seeds and upper pulp of the zucchini halves, leaving a $1/4$-rim around the edges.

2. In a large skillet over medium heat, warm 2 tablespoons of the olive oil and add the garlic, stirring with a wooden spoon, until it just starts to turn golden, about 2 minutes.

3. Add the shallots, oregano, nutmeg, and paprika, and cook until translucent, about another 2 minutes.

4. Add the tomatoes and continue to cook, until you have a fragrant mixture. Transfer to a plate and let it cool completely.

5. In a medium bowl, combine together the ricotta, $1/2$ cup of the Parmesan, $1/2$ cup of the bread crumbs, parsley, and egg yolks. Fold in the cooled onion mixture and season with salt and pepper.

6. Preheat the oven to 350°F.

7. Brush the insides of the zucchinis with another 2 tablespoons of olive oil and season with salt and pepper. Arrange the zucchini on a baking sheet covered with aluminum foil; lay the zucchinis facing up on the baking sheet and roast them in the oven until a knife inserted shows it is just tender, but not too tender, about 5 to 7 minutes.

8. Remove the zucchini from the oven and let them cool slightly. Fill each half with the ricotta mixture, mounding lightly, but not over spilling around the edges.

9. Sprinkle each zucchini with the remaining $1/4$ cup Parmesan cheese and the remaining $1/4$ cup bread crumbs, and drizzle another 2 tablespoons olive oil on top. Return them to the oven and bake until the top is lightly browned, another 10 to 15 minutes. Serve hot.

Desserts

Healthy Brigadeiro   201

Gluten-Free Brazil Nut Brownie   202

Pistachio Cake   205

Gluten-Free Pistachio and White Chocolate Tart   207

Molten Coconut Cake   209

Gluten-Free Guava Paste Thumbprint Cookies   211

Tapioca Pearl Pudding   212

Passion Fruit Eton Mess   215

Flourless Coco Nut Raspberry Cake   217

Roasted Pineapple   219

Pistachio Cake

Although pistachios are not immediately associated with Latin cooking, they are quite present in the São Paulo region in Brazil, where there is a huge Mediterranean influence and Lebanese, Turkish, and Syrian cuisines are quite popular. I used to eat pistachio cake on my day trips to São Paulo, in my previous life as a private banker. With memories of a frenetic city, important business lunches, and delicious food guiding me (food was my passion back then already, I just didn't know it), I decided to develop a gluten-free recipe that would take me back to those days. This cake is delicious served plain, or if you are planning to serve as a composed dessert, some strawberries or a sorbet will go nicely. You can find almond paste in any regular grocery store. Two brands that I use regularly are Odense and Solo. As for the pistachio paste, I used Love N' Bake for this recipe. **Serves 6 to 8**

2 tablespoons pistachio paste

1³⁄₄ (12-ounce) tube almond paste

12 tablespoons butter, at room temperature

4 eggs, at room temperature

3 tablespoons organic cane sugar

¹⁄₂ teaspoon almond extract

¹⁄₂ teaspoon vanilla extract

³⁄₄ cup + 1 tablespoon gluten-free flour, sifted

Confectioner's sugar, for serving

Equipment: one 9-inch round cake pan, greased, line with parchment paper, and greased again. Or the same for the 9 x 13-inch baking pan.

1. Center a rack in the middle of the oven and preheat to 350°F.

2. In the bowl of a food processor combine the pistachio paste and almond paste and beat just to break it up. Add the butter and pulse just until butter is well incorporated, light and airy.

3. Place the eggs and sugar in the bowl of an electric mixer. Set the bowl over a pan of simmering water (bowl should not touch water) and heat just until lukewarm to the touch, whisking constantly with a long whisk to prevent curdling. Bring the bowl to the mixer and attach the whisk beater. Start beating on low speed, gradually increasing to high speed. Beat on high until mixture has thickened, whitened, and tripled in volume, about 5 minutes. Add the vanilla and almond extract and continue beating.

4. Using a rubber spatula, add the pistachio paste mixture into the egg mixture and fold well, trying to keep the batter as light as possible (though it will deflate a little).

5. Add the gluten-free flour and incorporate with a rubber spatula until it's just mixed.

6. Pour the batter into the prepared pan and smooth the top with an off-set spatula. Bake the cake until golden brown and the sides pull away from the pan, around 25 minutes. Transfer to a rack and let rest for 10 minutes before unmolding. Cool completely and dust with powdered sugar before serving.

Gluten-Free Pistachio and White Chocolate Tart

The combination of white chocolate and pistachios has an international appeal that made me want to explore. It took a few months to develop this recipe because it had to be perfect and perform beautifully in the kitchens of any home cook. Mission accomplished. Creating and redesigning this recipe with a gluten-free tart crust reminds me of a powerful fact: that everything can be re-imagined, re-invented, and grains and starches can be a precious source. This tart is an elegant option for a special occasion, so go ahead and let your baking dreams shine! **Serves 10**

For the Gluten-Free Dough:

½ cup rice flour
⅓ cup cornstarch
⅓ cup ground almonds (or ground pistachios)
⅓ cup confectioner's sugar
¼ teaspoon xanthan gum
6 tablespoons cold butter
2 eggs (one for egg wash)

For the Pistachio Mousse:

¾ cup heavy cream
½ cup cream cheese, at room temperature
¼ cup + 2 tablespoons pistachio paste (I used Love N' Bake)
1 tablespoon light brown sugar
1 teaspoon vanilla extract

For the White Chocolate Ganache:

¼ cup + 2 tablespoons heavy cream
4 ounces white chocolate, well chopped
¼ cup pistachios, chopped to garnish

Equipment: 9-inch fluted tart mold

1. **Prepare the Dough:** combine the rice flour, cornstarch, ground almonds, confectioner's sugar, and xanthan gum in the bowl of an electric mixer or food processor. Little by little add the cold butter on low speed until it looks like coarse sand.

2. Beat one egg lightly with a fork, and add it, mixing slowly until a ball of dough forms. Transfer the dough to plastic wrap, flatten it, and wrap it tight. Dough can be prepared up to 5 days ahead of time, or frozen for 2 months.

3. Working on a starched surface (cornstarch or rice flour), roll the dough about 1/16-inch thick, lifting the dough often and dusting more starch as necessary, constantly turning the dough. Roll the dough up and around the rolling pin and unmold onto the tart mold, fitting into the bottom and sides, and patching as needed. Chill for at least 30 minutes.

4. **Bake the Crust:** Heat the oven to 350°F. Prick the dough all over the bottom and place inside it a circle of parchment paper slightly larger than the tart mold; fill this up with pie weights or dried beans. Bake the tart until the edges are lightly golden brown, about 12 minutes. Lift parchment and remove beans; return tart to the oven, and bake for an additional 7 to 10 minutes, until the crust is golden brown. Beat the remaining egg. Brush the crust

(Continued on next page)

with egg wash and return to the oven one more time until lightly golden brown, about 5 minutes more. Cool completely.

5. **Prepare the Pistachio Mousse:** In the bowl of an electric mixer fitted with the whisk attachment, whip the heavy cream to soft peaks. Using a rubber spatula, scrape into a smaller bowl and chill.

6. Using the same bowl fitted with the paddle attachment, place the cream cheese, pistachio paste, light brown sugar, and vanilla extract, and beat well until homogeneous. Stop the machine occasionally to scrape the sides of the bowl with a rubber spatula.

7. Remove the bowl from the machine and use a rubber spatula to incorporate the whipped cream into the mousse, folding carefully until it's all blended.

8. Using an off-set spatula, spread the mousse onto the cooled crust, making sure it's nice and flat. Chill for at least one hour before you make the ganache.

9. **Prepare the Ganache:** Place the chocolate in a stainless-steel bowl. In a small saucepan, bring the heavy cream just to a boil and immediately pour it over the chocolate. Stir the mixture carefully with a rubber spatula, starting from the center of the bowl, gradually incorporating the whole mixture until it's just blended. Don't over-mix it or the ganache will break. Don't wait too long either; you want to work while the ganache is still hot and spreadable. Pour the ganache over the mousse filling and spread to the edges of the pastry by carefully tilting the tart. Refrigerate the tart uncovered for at least 2 hours. Tart can be prepared up to 5 days ahead. If so, wrap the tart in plastic wrap after 2 hours of chilling.

10. Remove the tart from the refrigerator at least 30 minutes before serving. To unmold the tart, lift the bottom and tart should easily come out of the pan. Insert a long metal spatula between the crust and the bottom, and transfer to a nice, large plate. Dip a knife into hot water before cutting each slice, cleaning the edges of the knife between slices to make clean cuts.

Molten Coconut Cake

Molten cake, with its impressive rich, oozy center, has long been something I love to bake. This version with coconut is healthier but just as rich, moist, and sexy as the others—I love to serve it with a lime sorbet, but even plain is so good. **Serves 6**

1 (14-ounce) can organic
    sweetened condensed milk
1 cup coconut milk
1 cup unsweetened dried
    coconut, shredded
8 tablespoons (1 stick)
    unsalted butter (more for
    the molds), cut into cubes
2 whole eggs + 2 egg yolks
1/8 teaspoon salt
1 teaspoon vanilla extract
1/4 cup gluten-free flour, sifted
    (plus more for the molds)

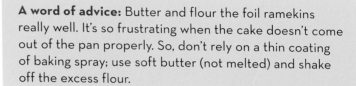

A word of advice: Butter and flour the foil ramekins really well. It's so frustrating when the cake doesn't come out of the pan properly. So, don't rely on a thin coating of baking spray; use soft butter (not melted) and shake off the excess flour.

1. Preheat oven to 350° F. Butter and flour six ramekins or reusable foil cups. Shake off the excess flour.

2. Place the sweetened condensed milk, coconut milk, and grated coconut in a saucepan, over medium heat. Whisk constantly until the mixture begins to bubble. Lower the heat and keep whisking until the batter has thickened, about 7 minutes. You are looking for a fudgy batter, thick and dense. Transfer to a bowl without scraping the pan.

3. Add the butter and whisk until melted and incorporated. Cool down to room temperature.

4. In a separate bowl, beat together the eggs, egg yolks, and salt. Add the vanilla.

5. Add the egg mixture into the coconut mixture and mix well with a spatula.

6. Add the gluten-free flour and mix just until blended.

7. Carefully pour the batter into the prepared foil cups or ramekins, filling almost to the top. Bake in the oven for 7 to 9 minutes. The cake won't rise nor turn golden brown during baking time—you know it's done when the edges are firm, but the center is still jiggly. Invert onto a dessert plate and serve with lemon sorbet.

Gluten-Free Guava Paste Thumbprint Cookies

When it comes to thumbprint cookies, the possibilities are endless. There are so many types of nuts and jellies. Over the years, I have tried dozens of combinations; some are great, some are good, and some are just boring.

This version is a Latin-inspired gluten-free cookie; I use guava paste but you can also use quince paste. I always find the baking part of thumbprint cookies a little challenging, because as hard as I try to create the perfect indentation, it tends to lose its shape in the oven. So, during baking time, make sure to rotate the pan, and re-enforce that indention by using a teaspoon. **Makes about 40 cookies**

½ cup rice flour
⅓ cup cornstarch
⅓ cup ground almonds (or ground pistachios)
⅓ cup confectioner's sugar
¼ teaspoon xanthan gum
6 tablespoons cold butter
2 eggs (one for egg wash)
1 cup guava paste
Few drops of lemon juice (optional)
Confectioner's sugar, for dusting

1. Combine the rice flour, cornstarch, ground almonds, confectioner's sugar, and xanthan gum in the bowl of an electric mixer or food processor. Little by little add the cold butter on low speed, until it looks like coarse sand.

2. Beat one egg lightly with a fork and add this, mixing slowly, until a ball of dough forms. Transfer the dough to plastic wrap, flatten it, and wrap it tight. Dough can be prepared up to 5 days ahead of time, or frozen for 2 months.

3. Preheat the oven to 350°F. Line two baking sheets with silicone mats.

4. Working with a tablespoon of dough at a time, roll between the palms of your hand to form small balls and place them 2 inches apart on the baking sheets. Use your pinkie, or the end of a wooden spoon, to press a hole in the center of each cookie. Be careful not to go all the way down to the baking sheet. Bake until slightly colored, about 14 minutes, rotating the sheet halfway through.

5. Remove the baking sheets from the oven and let them cool for 2 minutes before transferring to a wire rack. Once cool, sprinkle confectioner's sugar on top.

6. Place the guava paste in a saucepan over low heat and add just a few drops of water to melt the paste to the consistency of jam. Add a few drops of lemon juice to balance the sweetness (optional). You want to fill the cookies while the jam is still warm, so that it hardens inside the cookie. Fill the indentations of all cookies with enough warm guava jam to come to the level with the tops. Cool to room temperature.

Tapioca Pearl Pudding

When I graduated from cooking school, I went to work at La Caravelle, a legendary restaurant in New York City, with Eric Di Domenico, a talented French chef who always had a flair for Latin flavors. This recipe is inspired by a dinner I prepared with Eric in which he served a coconut tapioca pudding with a medley of tropical fruit cut into brunoise size (small dice).

It serves a lot of people, and it's one of those recipes easy to prepare ahead of time, even up to 5 days. You can keep it in a plastic container in the fridge and there is absolutely nothing to do, other than scooping out into ramekins (or a mold ring) and placing the fruit salad on top.

Look at the tapioca pudding as a blank canvas. While I love this combination of tropical fruit, you can also use others, like passion fruit pulp, or berries, or herb syrups, coconut tuilles, lime sorbet, coconut sorbet, or any other creation of your own.

This recipe is not too sweet and not too filling, and quite refreshing. About the serving vessels: once the pudding is cold, it's quite malleable. You can choose to serve in glass ramekins, or cups, or even removable rings. It all depends on the presentation you want to create. **Serves 10 to 12**

For the Pudding:

1⅓ cups small tapioca pearls
2 cups whole milk
1 (12-ounce) can evaporated milk
3 cups unsweetened coconut milk
1 cup organic cane sugar
Pinch salt

For the Fruit Brunoise:

2 kiwis
1 mango
½ pineapple
Mint sprigs, for garnish

1. **Prepare the Pudding**: Soak the tapioca in a bowl with plenty of cold water and refrigerate for at least 8 hours or overnight, until the pearls look glossy and translucent.

2. Pour the milk, evaporated milk, and coconut milk in a large saucepan (choose a really large pan, giving you plenty of room to stir the pudding), along with the sugar and pinch of salt, and bring it to a boil.

3. Meanwhile, drain the tapioca pearls over a colander and shake off any excess liquid.

4. Add the pearls to the milk mixture, reduce the heat to low, and simmer gently, stirring constantly with a wooden spoon, until the tapioca pearls are soft, about 10 minutes. If you're tempted to taste the pudding at this point, it will taste too sweet; once it's chilled, the taste will adjust. Also, don't fret if the pudding seems too liquid after simmering. As the pudding chills in the fridge, it will firm up to a beautiful consistency.

5. Pour the pudding into a bowl or plastic container and chill completely for at least 4 hours, preferably overnight. Keep it covered. You can prepare the pudding at this point up to 5 days ahead.

6. **Prepare the Fruit Brunoise:** Using a serrated knife, cut the kiwi, mango, and pineapple into small dice (*brunoise*) and combine everything in a bowl. It should look bright and colorful. Scoop some tapioca pudding into ramekins, applying gentle pressure to fit the ramekins; you might use a spoon or off-set spatula. Top with fruit *brunoise* and garnish with mint.

Passion Fruit Eton Mess

The exotic passion fruit is not exotic at all in Latin America; it's as common as strawberries here in the US. As a good Latin mama, I love using tropical fruit in my American kitchen, which is no longer difficult to find. Eton Mess, a classic British dessert (the name comes from Eton College, a boarding school in England, where this delicious dessert was introduced) is typically composed of meringue, fruit, and whipped cream. "Latinize me!," I heard it screaming to me. The result is a most joyful collection of flavors and textures that all work together and delight with every spoonful. Don't be scared to see the many components; the only component that will take you more than 5 minutes to prepare is the passion fruit curd (okay, it takes about 20 minutes). Everything else is a breeze to prepare. No kidding. If you want to make this dessert for a dinner party, you can prepare everything ahead of time and assemble just before serving. My advice is that you make the passion fruit curd, syrup, and yogurt ahead of time, and keep them all covered in plastic containers in the fridge. It is very important that these components are cold when assembling the dessert. The vanilla meringue and chia seeds should be kept at room temp. **Serves 6**

For the Passion Fruit Sauce:
½ cup turbinado sugar
½ cup plus 2 tablespoons passion fruit puree

For the Yogurt:
1 cup natural Greek yogurt (5%)
1 teaspoon vanilla extract
1 tablespoon honey

For the Passion Fruit Curd:
½ cup passion fruit puree
⅓ cup organic cane sugar
2 eggs
1 gelatin sheet or
  ½ teaspoon, bloomed in
  2 tablespoons of water
8 tablespoons unsalted butter, slightly cold, cut into cubes
12 store-bought vanilla meringue cookies, broken in pieces
3 tablespoons chia seeds, for garnish

1. **Prepare the Passion Fruit Sauce:** Place the sugar and passion fruit puree in a saucepan and cook over low heat, whisking constantly and slowly until all sugar is dissolved and it becomes the consistency of a syrup. Remove from the pan, transfer to a container, and let it cool completely.

2. **Prepare the Yogurt:** In a bowl, whisk together yogurt, vanilla, and honey until it's all blended.

3. **Prepare the Passion Fruit Curd:** Put the passion fruit puree, sugar, and eggs in a medium saucepan and cook, whisking constantly over the lowest heat, until mixture thickens. Do not let it boil. Add the bloomed gelatin into the curd and whisk well.

4. Remove from the heat, transfer to a bowl, and let it cool to room temperature for at least 20 minutes. Transfer the curd to a blender and with the machine running, add the pieces of butter slowly until it emulsifies well, and the curd looks silky and creamy. Transfer to a container with a tight lid and keep refrigerated.

5. **Assemble:** In decorative glasses, layer a spoonful of the passion fruit curd and then a spoonful of the yogurt mixture. Sprinkle some meringue on top and add a small amount of sauce on top. Repeat once or twice, depending on the size of the glass, until full. Sprinkle some chia seeds on top. Serve immediately.

Roasted Pineapple

One of my biggest aha *moments with pineapple was when I was an intern pastry chef at Le Cirque 2000, a legendary New York City restaurant, under the amazing chef Jacques Torres (who is now Mr. Chocolate with stores all over the US). He used to prepare a whole roasted pineapple that awed costumers every time. I brought this idea to my home kitchen and serve it in small bowls. For a more composed dessert, you can serve with coconut sorbet, or with some healthy cookies on the side. The pineapple can be served cold, room temperature, or slightly warm. It's a flexible dessert and you can dress it up, or down.* **Serves 6 to 8**

1 ripe pineapple
³/₄ cup orange juice
¹/₄ cup lime juice
¹/₂ cup apricot jam
3 cinnamon sticks, broken
    in half
2 tablespoons cardamom
2–3 star anise

1. Preheat the oven to 350°F.

2. Using a serrated knife, cut the top and bottom off the pineapple, and cut to peel the fruit all around following the contour. Holding the pineapple in your hands, cut every dark spot remaining from the pineapple, until the fruit is nice and clean.

3. Cut the pineapple into 4 sections around the core and discard it. Place the pineapple sections in a 7 x 11-inch baking dish.

4. In a bowl, whisk together the orange juice, lime juice, and apricot jam. Pour the mixture over the pineapple and add the spices to the baking dish. Bake for 60 minutes, basting frequently (about every 20 minutes) until it's nice and fragrant and a little darker in color.

5. Remove from the oven and let the pineapple cool in the baking dish until it's warm enough to handle, about 30 minutes.

6. You can serve the pineapple right from the baking dish, and spoon into nice ramekins, along with some of the sauce left in the pan. Feel free to serve it plain or with coconut sorbet.

Acknowledgments

Writing cookbooks is a big passion and this one in particular represents a huge deal for me, as my work and my heart are completely aligned under healthy cooking. I find that cooking is moving for so many reasons. It is in the kitchen where the majority of our health destiny is determined, and this book is my own tribute to healthy cooking.

Thanks to Max Sinsheimer for believing in me from the very beginning and guiding me through the whole process. To Leah Zarra, my editor at Skyhorse, for having the vision for this book and for being a wonderful editor.

Thanks to the many photographers who collaborated with me over the years, including Michelle Fonseca, Diego Batista, Marcela Falci, Ricardo de Mattos, and Luciano Bogado. It's an honor to feature your work in this book and I cannot thank you enough for so many beautiful photos!

Thanks to all my team at America's Diabetes Challenge, including Mary, Kristen, Kristin, Lexi, Julia, Samantha, Conrod, and a team that's so big that all the names would not fit in here. Working for this cause gave a new meaning to my life and my career, and fills my heart with the most noble purpose.

Thanks to my dear friends who I have the joy to cook for in my dining room, or bring recipes to yours and talk for hours about life and food.

Thanks to my super talented sister-in-law Fernanda Benzaquen, for creating the most beautiful photo boards; to my brother Jimmy for your continuous love and support; and your beautiful children Valentina and Nicky.

Thanks to my dear Jose Alberto Zusman, for twenty plus years together and going strong.

To my parents Selma and Salomon Benzaquen, thanks for loving me unconditionally and ensuring I came into this world full of love. And to my family, I just cannot find words to express how much I love cooking for you and how proud I am of you! Thanks to my husband Dean, for sitting with me in the kitchen to keep me company, and for all your love always. And for Thomas and Bianca for being the most loving son and daughter I could ever ask for. Your presence in this world fills my heart with joy and makes me want to be a better woman every day.

To all of my friends—online and in life—followers, cooking students and enthusiasts who attend my cooking classes, ask me for recipes, give me ideas, share my posts, comment in my blog, and help me create a community. I am honored to have the opportunity to encourage you all to cook and laugh in your own kitchen and generate health for your own family. This book is nothing but another opportunity to dream of health together. Because health is really the biggest success of all.

Conversion Charts

Metric and Imperial Conversions

(These conversions are rounded for convenience)

Ingredient	Cups/Tablespoons/Teaspoons	Ounces	Grams/Milliliters
Butter	1 cup/ 16 tablespoons/ 2 sticks	8 ounces	230 grams
Cheese, shredded	1 cup	4 ounces	110 grams
Cream cheese	1 tablespoon	0.5 ounce	14.5 grams
Cornstarch	1 tablespoon	0.3 ounce	8 grams
Flour, all-purpose	1 cup/1 tablespoon	4.5 ounces/0.3 ounce	125 grams/8 grams
Flour, whole wheat	1 cup	4 ounces	120 grams
Fruit, dried	1 cup	4 ounces	120 grams
Fruits or veggies, chopped	1 cup	5 to 7 ounces	145 to 200 grams
Fruits or veggies, pureed	1 cup	8.5 ounces	245 grams
Honey, maple syrup, or corn syrup	1 tablespoon	0.75 ounce	20 grams
Liquids: cream, milk, water, or juice	1 cup	8 fluid ounces	240 milliliters
Oats	1 cup	5.5 ounces	150 grams
Salt	1 teaspoon	0.2 ounce	6 grams
Spices: cinnamon, cloves, ginger, or nutmeg (ground)	1 teaspoon	0.2 ounce	5 milliliters
Sugar, brown, firmly packed	1 cup	7 ounces	200 grams
Sugar, white	1 cup/1 tablespoon	7 ounces/0.5 ounce	200 grams/12.5 grams
Vanilla extract	1 teaspoon	0.2 ounce	4 grams

Oven Temperatures

Fahrenheit	Celsius	Gas Mark
225°	110°	$\frac{1}{4}$
250°	120°	$\frac{1}{2}$
275°	140°	1
300°	150°	2
325°	160°	3
350°	180°	4
375°	190°	5
400°	200°	6
425°	220°	7
450°	230°	8

Index

A

açaí, 13
Açaí, Power Bowl, 37
Addictive Cucumba Salad, 109
aji amarillo paste
    Addictive Cucumba Salad, 109
    Broccoli Fajitas with Cashew, 192
almond butter
    Be My Date Bowl, 35
    Survivor Bowl, 39
almond milk
    Açaí Power Bowl, 37
    Be My Date Bowl, 35
    Mango Lassi, 39
    Pumpkin Protein Shake, 41
almond paste
    Pistachio Cake, 205
almonds
    Bok Choy Salad with Sunflower Seeds, 81
    Gluten-Free Guava Paste, 211
    Gluten-Free Pistachio and White Chocolate
        Tart, 207–208
    Jeweled Carrot Rice, 174
    Kale Gorgonzola Salad, 100
    Romesco Sauce, 61
    Scrambled Eggs with Romesco Sauce, 60
apples
    Wheatberry Waldorf Salad, 89
apricot
    Moroccan Rubbed Red Snapper with Apricot
        and Hazelnut Sauce, 152–153
    Papa Coco Cash Bowl, 34
    Tropical Granola, 43
apricot jam
    Roasted Pineapple, 219
Arroz con Pollo, 112–113
arugula
    Butternut Mash with Arugula Pesto, 187
    Kale Gnocchi, 74–75
    Watermelon Carpaccio with Feta Cheese,
        Olives, Cilantro and Arugula, 107
avocado, 13
    Brazilian Guacamole, 47
    Whole Wheat Fusilli with Chicken and Avocado
        Cashew Pesto, 178–179

B

bacon
    turkey
        Baião de Dois (Stir Fry Brazilian Style), 175
        Quinoa Risotto with Peas and Turkey Bacon,
            181
Baião de Dois (Stir Fry Brazilian Style), 175
banana
    Açaí Power Bowl, 37
    Be My Date Bowl, 35
    Fish Moqueca with Banana, Cashews, and
        Cilantro, 162–163
    Papa Coco Cash Bowl, 34
    Pumpkin Protein Shake, 41
    Survivor Bowl, 39
    Tropical Granola, 43
barley
    Chicken Barley Stew, 124–125
beans, 13
    black
        Black Bean Burger, 190–191
        Hearty Black Bean Soup, 97
        Rice and Beans the Modern Way, 177
        Sweet Potato and Green Bean Salad, 95
    kidney
        Feijao Tropeiro, 172–173
    string
        Sweet Potato and Green Bean Salad, 95
bell peppers
    Baião de Dois (Stir Fry Brazilian Style), 175
    Brazilian Guacamole, 47
    Carrot Ginger Smoothie, 32
    Ceviche with Tiger's Milk, 73

Chicken, Cashew, and Red Pepper Stir Fry, 126
Coffee-Rubbed Chicken Breast with Corn
    Salsa, 133
Hearts of Palm Ceviche, 67
Huevos Cubanos, 69
Mexican Creamed Corn, 197
Picadillo de Pollo, 139
Rice and Beans the Modern Way, 177
Romesco Sauce, 61
Ropa Vieja de Pollo, 115–116
Turkey Sausage with Bell Peppers, 118
Be My Date Bowl, 35
Black Bean Burger, 190–191
blueberries
    Be My Date Bowl, 35
Bluebie Orange Smoothie, 31
Bok Choy Salad with Sunflower Seeds, 81
Braised Chicken with Fennel and Oranges, 142–143
Brazilian Guacamole, 47
Brazil Nut Latte, 41
Brazil nuts, 14
    Flourless Coco Nut Raspberry Cake, 217
    Gluten-Free Brazil Nut Brownie, 202
    Tropical Granola, 43
bread
    Romesco Sauce, 61
    Salmon Cakes with Coconut Ginger Sauce,
      157–158
Broccoli Fajitas with Cashew, 192
Butternut Mash with Arugula Pesto, 187

C
cacao nibs
    Açaí Power Bowl, 37
    Healthy Brigadeiro, 201
cachaça
    Grilled Shrimp with a Caipirinha Vinaigrette, 151
cantaloupe
    Carrot Ginger Smoothie, 32
capers
    Fish Veracruz, 167
    Ropa Vieja de Pollo, 115–116
cardamom
    Mango Lassi, 39
    Roasted Pineapple, 219
Carrot Ginger Smoothie, 32
carrots
    Chicken Tamale Pie, 119–121

Hearty Black Bean Soup, 97
Jeweled Carrot Rice, 174
Picadillo de Pollo, 139
cashew butter
    Papa Coco Cash Bowl, 34
cashews
    Broccoli Fajitas with Cashew, 192
    Chicken, Cashew, and Red Pepper Stir Fry, 126
    Fish Moqueca with Banana, Cashews, and
      Cilantro, 162–163
    Papa Coco Cash Bowl, 34
    Tropical Granola, 43
    Whole Wheat Fusilli with Chicken and Avocado
      Cashew Pesto, 178–179
cayenne, 20
celery, 14
    Chicken Tamale Pie, 119–121
    Hearty Black Bean Soup, 97
    Picadillo de Pollo, 139
    Salmon Marinated in Celery Juice, 57
    Spinach Soup with Egg Salad, 90
    Wheatberry Waldorf Salad, 89
Celery Salad, 105
Ceviche with Tiger's Milk, 73
chayote, 14–15
Chayote Salad with Quinoa and Mustard
    Vinaigrette, 84
cheese
    Boucheron
      Scrambled Eggs with Romesco Sauce, 60
    feta
      Baião de Dois (Stir Fry Brazilian Style), 175
      Grilled Eggplant with Minas Cheese and
        Cilantro, 87
      Mexican Creamed Corn, 197
    Gorgonzola
      Gorgonzola Mousse, 49
      Kale Gorgonzola Salad, 100
    Minas
      Spinach Minas Quiche, 62
    mozzarella
      Spinach Mushroom Quesadilla, 71
      Tapioca Crepe with Tomato Mozzarella, 55
    Parmesan
      Butternut Mash with Arugula Pesto, 187
      Flaxseed-Crusted Tamale Cakes, 188
      Gluten-Free Cheese Crackers, 65
      Hearts of Palm and Spinach Dip, 50

Kale Gnocchi, 74–75
Quinoa Risotto with Peas and Turkey Bacon, 181
Ricotta-Stuffed Zucchini, 198
Shiitake Carpaccio, 83
Sopa Seca, 99
Spinach Minas Quiche, 62
Yucca Latkes, 183
Pecorino Velathri, 105
queso-blanco, 21
Baião de Dois (Stir Fry Brazilian Style), 175
Chicken Tortilla Soup, 101–103
Grilled Eggplant with Minas Cheese and Cilantro, 87
Mexican Creamed Corn, 197
Orange Salad with Pumpkin Seeds and Crumbled Queso-Blanco, 93
Sopa Seca, 99
Warm Cucumber Chicken Salad, 117
Watermelon Carpaccio with Feta Cheese, Olives, Cilantro and Arugula, 107
ricotta
Gorgonzola Mousse, 49
Chia-Crusted Salmon with Passion Fruit Sauce, 169
chia seeds, 18
Chia-Crusted Salmon with Passion Fruit Sauce, 169
Papa Coco Cash Bowl, 34
Passion Fruit Eton Mess, 215
chicken, 15
Arroz con Pollo, 112–113
Baião de Dois (Stir Fry Brazilian Style), 175
Braised Chicken with Fennel and Oranges, 142–143
Chicken Tamale Pie, 119–121
Chicken Tortilla Soup, 101–103
Grilled Chicken Drumstick with Orange Glaze, 135
Picadillo de Pollo, 139
Ropa Vieja de Pollo, 115–116
Warm Cucumber Chicken Salad, 117
Whole Wheat Fusilli with Chicken and Avocado Cashew Pesto, 178–179
Chicken, Cashew, and Red Pepper Stir Fry, 126
Chicken Barley Stew, 124–125
Chicken in a Pot, 123
chicken sausage
Tortilla Espanola, 51

Chicken Stew with Tomatillos and Cilantro, 137
chicken stock, 8–9
Arroz con Pollo, 112–113
Baião de Dois (Stir Fry Brazilian Style), 175
Braised Chicken with Fennel and Oranges, 142–143
Chicken, Cashew, and Red Pepper Stir Fry, 126
Chicken Barley Stew, 124–125
Chicken Stew with Tomatillos and Cilantro, 137
Chicken Tortilla Soup, 101–103
Chicken with Peas and Potatoes, 127–128
Fish Veracruz, 167
Fish with Pepita Sauce, 161
Picadillo de Pollo, 139
Quinoa Risotto with Peas and Turkey Bacon, 181
Ropa Vieja de Pollo, 115–116
Spinach Soup with Egg Salad, 90
Turkey Sausage with Bell Peppers, 118
Chicken Tamale Pie, 119–121
Chicken Tortilla Soup, 101–103
Chicken with Peas and Potatoes, 127–128
chickpeas
Sopa Seca, 99
chipotle chiles
Chicken Tortilla Soup, 101–103
chives
Chayote Salad with Quinoa and Mustard Vinaigrette, 84
Chicken, Cashew, and Red Pepper Stir Fry, 126
Coffee-Rubbed Chicken Breast with Corn Salsa, 133
Sardines with Tomato Olive Salsa, 168
chocolate, 15–16
Gluten-Free Brazil Nut Brownie, 202
Healthy Brigadeiro, 201
white
Gluten-Free Pistachio and White Chocolate Tart, 207–208
cilantro
Black Bean Burger, 190–191
Brazilian Guacamole, 47
Broccoli Fajitas with Cashew, 192
Ceviche with Tiger's Milk, 73
Chia-Crusted Salmon with Passion Fruit Sauce, 169
Chicken Stew with Tomatillos and Cilantro, 137
Chicken Tortilla Soup, 101–103

Coffee-Rubbed Chicken Breast with Corn
  Salsa, 133
Farofa, 183
Fish Moqueca with Banana, Cashews, and
  Cilantro, 162–163
Fish with Pepita Sauce, 161
Flaxseed-Crusted Tamale Cakes, 188
Grilled Chicken Drumstick with Orange
  Glaze, 135
Grilled Eggplant with Minas Cheese and
  Cilantro, 87
Grilled Shrimp with a Caipirinha Vinaigrette, 151
Hearts of Palm Ceviche, 67
Mexican Creamed Corn, 197
Orange Salad with Pumpkin Seeds and
  Crumbled Queso-Blanco, 93
Picadillo de Pollo, 139
Rice and Beans the Modern Way, 177
Salmon Cakes with Coconut Ginger Sauce,
  157–158
Tacos Pico de Gallo, 195
Whole Wheat Fusilli with Chicken and Avocado
  Cashew Pesto, 178–179
cinnamon
  Be My Date Bowl, 35
  Brazil Nut Latte, 41
  Moroccan Rubbed Red Snapper with Apricot
    and Hazelnut Sauce, 152–153
  Survivor Bowl, 39
  Tropical Granola, 43
cocoa nibs, 16
cocoa powder
  Açaí Power Bowl, 37
  Be My Date Bowl, 35
  Healthy Brigadeiro, 201
  Turkey with Mole Sauce, 129–131
coconut, 16
  Flourless Coco Nut Raspberry Cake, 217
  Papa Coco Cash Bowl, 34
  Tropical Granola, 43
coconut milk
  Fish Moqueca with Banana, Cashews, and
    Cilantro, 162–163
  Healthy Brigadeiro, 201
  Molten Chocolate Cake, 209
  Papa Coco Cash Bowl, 34
  Survivor Bowl, 39
coconut water

Bluebie Orange Smoothie, 31
Cucumba Lemonade, 33
Minty Lemony Agua Fresca, 29
Orange Fennel Agua Fresca, 29
coffee, instant
  Gluten-Free Brazil Nut Brownie, 202
Coffee-Rubbed Chicken Breast with Corn Salsa,
  133
cookies, vanilla meringue
  Passion Fruit Eton Mess, 215
coriander
  Chicken Stew with Tomatillos and Cilantro, 137
  Coffee-Rubbed Chicken Breast with Corn
    Salsa, 133
  Papas y Salsicha Criolla, 147
  Picadillo de Pollo, 139
  Ropa Vieja de Pollo, 115–116
  Spiced Swordfish Skewers, 159
corn
  Coffee-Rubbed Chicken Breast with Corn
    Salsa, 133
  Flaxseed-Crusted Tamale Cakes, 188
  Mexican Creamed Corn, 197
crackers
  Gluten-Free Cheese Crackers, 65
cream
  Gluten-Free Pistachio and White Chocolate
    Tart, 207–208
  Scrambled Eggs with Romesco Sauce, 60
  Watercress Flan, 76–78
cream cheese
  Hearts of Palm and Spinach Dip, 50
Cucumba Lemonade, 33
cucumber
  Addictive Cucumba Salad, 109
  Brazilian Guacamole, 47
  Minty Lemony Agua Fresca, 29
  Warm Cucumber Chicken Salad, 117
cumin
  Chicken Stew with Tomatillos and Cilantro, 137
  Hearty Black Bean Soup, 97
  Moroccan Rubbed Red Snapper with Apricot
    and Hazelnut Sauce, 152–153
  Rice and Beans the Modern Way, 177
  Ropa Vieja de Pollo, 115–116
  Salmon Cakes with Coconut Ginger Sauce,
    157–158
  Sopa Seca, 99

D

dates, 16
  Be My Date Bowl, 35
dill
  Chayote Salad with Quinoa and Mustard
    Vinaigrette, 84
  Cucumba Lemonade, 33
  Fish Veracruz, 167
  Flaxseed-Crusted Tamale Cakes, 188
  Rice and Beans the Modern Way, 177
  Salmon Marinated in Celery Juice, 57
  Salmon with Pumpkin Sunflower Sauce, 155
  Tequila Gravlax, 59
  Warm Cucumber Chicken Salad, 117

E

eggplant, 17
  Fish with Eggplant and Tomato Sauce, 165–166
  Grilled Eggplant with Minas Cheese and
    Cilantro, 87
eggs, 17
  Spinach Soup with Egg Salad, 90
  Tortilla Espanola, 51

F

Farofa, 183
Feijao Tropeiro, 172–173
fennel
  Braised Chicken with Fennel and Oranges,
    142–143
  Orange Fennel Agua Fresca, 29
fish, 17
  Ceviche with Tiger's Milk, 73
  Chia-Crusted Salmon with Passion Fruit Sauce,
    169
  Fish Moqueca with Banana, Cashews, and
    Cilantro, 162–163
  Fish Veracruz, 167
  Fish with Eggplant and Tomato Sauce, 165–166
  Fish with Pepita Sauce, 161
  Moroccan Rubbed Red Snapper with Apricot
    and Hazelnut Sauce, 152–153
Fish Moqueca with Banana, Cashews, and Cilantro,
  162–163
fish stock
  Salmon Cakes with Coconut Ginger Sauce,
    157–158
Fish Veracruz, 167

Fish with Eggplant and Tomato Sauce, 165–166
Fish with Pepita Sauce, 161
Flaxseed-Crusted Tamale Cakes, 188
flax seeds, 18
Flourless Coco Nut Raspberry Cake, 217

G

garlic, 17–18
  Arroz con Pollo, 112–113
  Baião de Dois (Stir Fry Brazilian Style), 175
  Braised Chicken with Fennel and Oranges,
    142–143
  Butternut Mash with Arugula Pesto, 187
  Chicken, Cashew, and Red Pepper Stir Fry, 126
  Chicken in a Pot, 123
  Chicken Stew with Tomatillos and Cilantro, 137
  Chicken Tamale Pie, 119–121
  Chicken Tortilla Soup, 101–103
  Chicken with Peas and Potatoes, 127–128
  Coffee-Rubbed Chicken Breast with Corn
    Salsa, 133
  Farofa, 183
  Feijao Tropeiro, 172–173
  Fish Moqueca with Banana, Cashews, and
    Cilantro, 162–163
  Fish Veracruz, 167
  Hearts of Palm and Spinach Dip, 50
  Hearty Black Bean Soup, 97
  Huevos Cubanos, 69
  Picadillo de Pollo, 139
  Quinoa with Chicken Sausage and Mushrooms,
    144–145
  Rice and Beans the Modern Way, 177
  Ricotta-Stuffed Zucchini, 198
  Roasted Chicken Breast with Guava BBQ
    Sauce, 140–141
  Romesco Sauce, 61
  Ropa Vieja de Pollo, 115–116
  Salmon Cakes with Coconut Ginger Sauce,
    157–158
  Shiitake Carpaccio, 83
  Sopa Seca, 99
  Spiced Swordfish Skewers, 159
  Spinach Minas Quiche, 62
  Spinach Mushroom Quesadilla, 71
  Spinach Soup with Egg Salad, 90
  Tortilla Espanola, 51
  Turkey with Mole Sauce, 129–131

Watercress Flan, 76–78
Whole Wheat Fusilli with Chicken and Avocado
    Cashew Pesto, 178–179
ginger, 18
    Brazil Nut Latte, 41
    Carrot Ginger Smoothie, 32
    Chicken, Cashew, and Red Pepper Stir Fry, 126
    Fish Moqueca with Banana, Cashews, and
        Cilantro, 162–163
    Grilled Chicken Drumstick with Orange Glaze,
        135
    Moroccan Rubbed Red Snapper with Apricot
        and Hazelnut Sauce, 152–153
    Salmon Cakes with Coconut Ginger Sauce,
        157–158
    Salmon Marinated in Celery Juice, 57
    Spiced Swordfish Skewers, 159
Gluten-Free Brazil Nut Brownie, 202
Gluten-Free Cheese Crackers, 65
Gluten-Free Guava Paste, 211
Gluten-Free Pistachio and White Chocolate Tart,
    207–208
gnocchi
    Kale Gnocchi, 74–75
Gorgonzola Mousse, 49
granola
    Açaí Power Bowl, 37
    Be My Date Bowl, 35
    Survivor Bowl, 39
    Tropical Granola, 43
Grilled Chicken Drumstick with Orange Glaze, 135
Grilled Eggplant with Minas Cheese and Cilantro,
    87
Grilled Shrimp with a Caipirinha Vinaigrette, 151
guacamole
    Brazilian Guacamole, 47
guava paste
    Gluten-Free Guava Paste, 211
    Roasted Chicken Breast with Guava BBQ
        Sauce, 140–141

H
hazelnuts
    Moroccan Rubbed Red Snapper with Apricot
        and Hazelnut Sauce, 152–153
Healthy Brigadeiro, 201
hearts of palm, 18
Hearts of Palm and Spinach Salad, 85

Hearts of Palm Ceviche, 67
Hearts of Palm and Spinach Dip, 50
Hearty Black Bean Soup, 97
hemp seeds, 18
    Celery Salad, 105
    Orange Salad with Pumpkin Seeds and
        Crumbled Queso-Blanco, 93
    Survivor Bowl, 39
    Watermelon Carpaccio with Feta Cheese,
        Olives, Cilantro and Arugula, 107
honey
    Ceviche with Tiger's Milk, 73
    Grilled Chicken Drumstick with Orange
        Glaze, 135
    Mango Lassi, 39
    Orange Salad with Pumpkin Seeds and
        Crumbled Queso-Blanco, 93
    Pumpkin Protein Shake, 41
    Tropical Granola, 43
Huevos Cubanos, 69

J
jalapeño
    Broccoli Fajitas with Cashew, 192
Jeweled Carrot Rice, 174

K
kale, 18–19
    Feijao Tropeiro, 172–173
    Rice and Beans the Modern Way, 177
Kale Gnocchi, 74–75
Kale Gorgonzola Salad, 100

L
leeks
    Farofa, 183
lettuce
    Fish with Pepita Sauce, 161
    Kale Gnocchi, 74–75
lime
    Addictive Cucumba Salad, 109
    Arroz con Pollo, 112–113
    Ceviche with Tiger's Milk, 73
    Grilled Eggplant with Minas Cheese and
        Cilantro, 87
    Grilled Shrimp with a Caipirinha Vinaigrette, 151
    Hearts of Palm and Spinach Salad, 85
    Hearts of Palm Ceviche, 67

Mango Lassi, 39
Minty Lemony Agua Fresca, 29
Spiced Swordfish Skewers, 159

M

mango, 19
Mango Lassi, 39
manioc flour, 24
    Farofa, 183
    Feijao Tropeiro, 172–173
manioc meal, 24
manioc starch, 24
    Gluten-Free Cheese Crackers, 65
maple syrup
    Brazil Nut Latte, 41
matcha
    Survivor Bowl, 39
mayonnaise
    Broccoli Fajitas with Cashew, 192
    Hearts of Palm and Spinach Dip, 50
Mexican Creamed Corn, 197
microgreens
    Addictive Cucumba Salad, 109
mint
    Celery Salad, 105
    Ceviche with Tiger's Milk, 73
    Hearts of Palm Ceviche, 67
    Tapioca Pearl Pudding, 212
Minty Lemony Agua Fresca, 29
Molten Chocolate Cake, 209
Moroccan Rubbed Red Snapper with Apricot and
    Hazelnut Sauce, 152–153
mushrooms, 19
    Chicken Barley Stew, 124–125
    Quinoa with Chicken Sausage and Mushrooms,
      144–145
    Shiitake Carpaccio, 83
    Spinach Mushroom Quesadilla, 71
mustard
    Broccoli Fajitas with Cashew, 192
    Celery Salad, 105
    Chia-Crusted Salmon with Passion Fruit Sauce,
      169
    Chicken in a Pot, 123
    Hearts of Palm and Spinach Salad, 85
    Sweet Potato and Green Bean Salad, 95
    Wheatberry Waldorf Salad, 89

N

nutmeg
    Black Bean Burger, 190–191
    Butternut Mash with Arugula Pesto, 187
    Chicken Barley Stew, 124–125
    Chicken Tamale Pie, 119–121
    Chicken Tortilla Soup, 101–103
    Feijao Tropeiro, 172–173
    Flaxseed-Crusted Tamale Cakes, 188
    Hearts of Palm and Spinach Dip, 50
    Hearty Black Bean Soup, 97
    Huevos Cubanos, 69
    Papas y Salsicha Criolla, 147
    Picadillo de Pollo, 139
    Quinoa Risotto with Peas and Turkey Bacon, 181
    Quinoa with Chicken Sausage and Mushrooms,
      144–145
    Ropa Vieja de Pollo, 115–116
    Spinach Minas Quiche, 62
    Spinach Mushroom Quesadilla, 71
    Spinach Soup with Egg Salad, 90
    Tortilla Espanola, 51
    Turkey Sausage with Bell Peppers, 118
    Watercress Flan, 76–78
    Yucca Latkes, 183

O

oats, 43
Old Bay seasoning
    Salmon Cakes with Coconut Ginger Sauce,
      157–158
olives
    Jeweled Carrot Rice, 174
    Ropa Vieja de Pollo, 115–116
    Sardines with Tomato Olive Salsa, 168
    Watermelon Carpaccio with Feta Cheese,
      Olives, Cilantro and Arugula, 107
Orange Fennel Agua Fresca, 29
orange juice, 31
    Bluebie Orange Smoothie, 31
    Braised Chicken with Fennel and Oranges,
      142–143
    Ceviche with Tiger's Milk, 73
    Orange Salad with Pumpkin Seeds and
      Crumbled Queso-Blanco, 93
    Roasted Pineapple, 219
oranges, 19–20

Braised Chicken with Fennel and Oranges, 142–143
Broccoli Fajitas with Cashew, 192
Orange Salad with Pumpkin Seeds and Crumbled Queso-Blanco, 93
Orange Salad with Pumpkin Seeds and Crumbled Queso-Blanco, 93
oregano, 137
    Arroz con Pollo, 112–113
    Black Bean Burger, 190–191
    Chicken Barley Stew, 124–125
    Fish Veracruz, 167
    Picadillo de Pollo, 139
    Ricotta-Stuffed Zucchini, 198
    Sopa Seca, 99
    Spiced Swordfish Skewers, 159
    Turkey Sausage with Bell Peppers, 118

P

Papa Coco Cash Bowl, 34
Papas y Salsicha Criolla, 147
papayas, 20
    Papa Coco Cash Bowl, 34
    Sunny Smoothie, 31
paprika, 20
    Addictive Cucumba Salad, 109
    Arroz con Pollo, 112–113
    Baião de Dois (Stir Fry Brazilian Style), 175
    Chicken Barley Stew, 124–125
    Coffee-Rubbed Chicken Breast with Corn Salsa, 133
    Fish Veracruz, 167
    Huevos Cubanos, 69
    Moroccan Rubbed Red Snapper with Apricot and Hazelnut Sauce, 152–153
    Papas y Salsicha Criolla, 147
    Picadillo de Pollo, 139
    Quinoa with Chicken Sausage and Mushrooms, 144–145
    Ricotta-Stuffed Zucchini, 198
    Ropa Vieja de Pollo, 115–116
    Salmon Cakes with Coconut Ginger Sauce, 157–158
    Spinach Minas Quiche, 62
    Tortilla Espanola, 51
    Turkey Sausage with Bell Peppers, 118
passion fruit, 20
    Chia-Crusted Salmon with Passion Fruit Sauce, 169

Passion Fruit Eton Mess, 215
pasta
    Sopa Seca, 99
peanut butter
    Pumpkin Protein Shake, 41
peanuts
    Broccoli Fajitas with Cashew, 192
peas
    Chicken with Peas and Potatoes, 127–128
    Quinoa Risotto with Peas and Turkey Bacon, 181
pecans
    Wheatberry Waldorf Salad, 89
peppers, 13–14, 20
pesto
    Tapioca Crepe with Tomato Mozzarella, 55
    Whole Wheat Fusilli with Chicken and Avocado Cashew Pesto, 178–179
Picadillo de Pollo, 139
pineapple, 21
    Roasted Pineapple, 219
    Tapioca Pearl Pudding, 212
Pistachio Cake, 205
pistachios
    Gluten-Free Guava Paste, 211
    Gluten-Free Pistachio and White Chocolate Tart, 207–208
poblano pepper
    Fish with Pepita Sauce, 161
pomegranate
    Chayote Salad with Quinoa and Mustard Vinaigrette, 84
portion control, 10
potatoes
    Chicken Stew with Tomatillos and Cilantro, 137
    Chicken with Peas and Potatoes, 127–128
    Papas y Salsicha Criolla, 147
    Spinach Soup with Egg Salad, 90
    Tortilla Espanola, 51
pumpkin, 21
Pumpkin Protein Shake, 41
pumpkin seeds
    Fish with Pepita Sauce, 161
    Orange Salad with Pumpkin Seeds and Crumbled Queso-Blanco, 93
    Salmon with Pumpkin Sunflower Sauce, 155

Q

quesadilla
    Spinach Mushroom Quesadilla, 71
queso-blanco, 21
quinoa, 22
    Addictive Cucumba Salad, 109
    Chayote Salad with Quinoa and Mustard
        Vinaigrette, 84
    Quinoa Risotto with Peas and Turkey Bacon, 181
Quinoa Risotto with Peas and Turkey Bacon, 181
Quinoa with Chicken Sausage and Mushrooms,
    144–145

R

raisins
    Chicken in a Pot, 123
    Farofa, 183
    Tropical Granola, 43
raspberries
    Flourless Coco Nut Raspberry Cake, 217
red snapper
    Fish with Eggplant and Tomato Sauce, 165–166
    Moroccan Rubbed Red Snapper with Apricot
        and Hazelnut Sauce, 152–153
rice
    brown
        Arroz con Pollo, 112–113
        Baião de Dois (Stir Fry Brazilian Style), 175
    Jeweled Carrot Rice, 174
    wild
        Bok Choy Salad with Sunflower Seeds, 81
        Rice and Beans the Modern Way, 177
Rice and Beans the Modern Way, 177
ricotta
    Gorgonzola Mousse, 49
Ricotta-Stuffed Zucchini, 198
Roasted Chicken Breast with Guava BBQ Sauce,
    140–141
Roasted Pineapple, 219
Romesco Sauce, 61
    Scrambled Eggs with Romesco Sauce, 60
Ropa Vieja de Pollo, 115–116
rosemary
    Fish with Eggplant and Tomato Sauce, 165–166
    Gorgonzola Mousse, 49
    Roasted Chicken Breast with Guava BBQ
        Sauce, 140–141
    Turkey with Mole Sauce, 129–131

S

saffron
    Jeweled Carrot Rice, 174
    Watercress Flan, 76–78
salmon
    Chia-Crusted Salmon with Passion Fruit Sauce,
        169
    Tequila Gravlax, 59
Salmon Cakes with Coconut Ginger Sauce, 157–158
Salmon Marinated in Celery Juice, 57
Salmon with Pumpkin Sunflower Sauce, 155
sardines
    Sardines with Tomato Olive Salsa, 168
Sardines with Tomato Olive Salsa, 168
sausage
    chicken
        Arroz con Pollo, 112–113
        Baião de Dois (Stir Fry Brazilian Style), 175
        Feijao Tropeiro, 172–173
        Papas y Salsicha Criolla, 147
        Quinoa with Chicken Sausage and
            Mushrooms, 144–145
        Tortilla Espanola, 51
    turkey
        Turkey Sausage with Bell Peppers, 118
scallions
    Arroz con Pollo, 112–113
    Baião de Dois (Stir Fry Brazilian Style), 175
    Black Bean Burger, 190–191
    Bok Choy Salad with Sunflower Seeds, 81
    Chicken Stew with Tomatillos and Cilantro, 137
    Chicken Tamale Pie, 119–121
    Farofa, 183
    Feijao Tropeiro, 172–173
    Fish with Pepita Sauce, 161
    Grilled Eggplant with Minas Cheese and
        Cilantro, 87
    Picadillo de Pollo, 139
    Salmon Cakes with Coconut Ginger Sauce,
        157–158
    Sopa Seca, 99
    Sweet Potato and Green Bean Salad, 95
    Tortilla Espanola, 51
    Wheatberry Waldorf Salad, 89
Scrambled Eggs with Romesco Sauce, 60
sea bass
    Fish Moqueca with Banana, Cashews, and
        Cilantro, 162–163

serrano chiles
    Tacos Pico de Gallo, 195
sesame seeds
    Addictive Cucumba Salad, 109
    Hearts of Palm and Spinach Salad, 85
    Shiitake Carpaccio, 83
    Spiced Swordfish Skewers, 159
shallot
    Chia-Crusted Salmon with Passion Fruit Sauce, 169
    Chicken with Peas and Potatoes, 127–128
    Coffee-Rubbed Chicken Breast with Corn Salsa, 133
    Orange Salad with Pumpkin Seeds and Crumbled Queso-Blanco, 93
    Ricotta-Stuffed Zucchini, 198
    Salmon Cakes with Coconut Ginger Sauce, 157–158
    Salmon with Pumpkin Sunflower Sauce, 155
    Sopa Seca, 99
    Spinach Minas Quiche, 62
    Spinach Mushroom Quesadilla, 71
    Spinach Soup with Egg Salad, 90
    Sweet Potato and Green Bean Salad, 95
    Tortilla Espanola, 51
    Warm Cucumber Chicken Salad, 117
    Watercress Flan, 76–78
    Watermelon Carpaccio with Feta Cheese, Olives, Cilantro and Arugula, 107
    Whole Wheat Fusilli with Chicken and Avocado Cashew Pesto, 178–179
Shiitake Carpaccio, 83
shrimp
    Grilled Shrimp with a Caipirinha Vinaigrette, 151
shrimp stock
    Fish Moqueca with Banana, Cashews, and Cilantro, 162–163
sofrito, 8
Sopa Seca, 99
sour cream
    Chayote Salad with Quinoa and Mustard Vinaigrette, 84
    Gorgonzola Mousse, 49
    Hearts of Palm and Spinach Dip, 50
    Spinach Soup with Egg Salad, 90
    Watercress Flan, 76–78
soy sauce
    Bok Choy Salad with Sunflower Seeds, 81

Brazilian Guacamole, 47
Chicken, Cashew, and Red Pepper Stir Fry, 126
Hearts of Palm and Spinach Salad, 85
Roasted Chicken Breast with Guava BBQ Sauce, 140–141
Salmon Cakes with Coconut Ginger Sauce, 157–158
Salmon with Pumpkin Sunflower Sauce, 155
Shiitake Carpaccio, 83
Spiced Swordfish Skewers, 159
spinach
    Hearts of Palm and Spinach Salad, 85
    Hearts of Palm and Spinach Dip, 50
    Sopa Seca, 99
    Spinach Minas Quiche, 62
    Spinach Soup with Egg Salad, 90
    Survivor Bowl, 39
Spinach Minas Quiche, 62
Spinach Mushroom Quesadilla, 71
Spinach Soup with Egg Salad, 90
squash. See also pumpkin
    chayote, 14–15
star anise
    Roasted Pineapple, 219
sunflower seeds
    Bok Choy Salad with Sunflower Seeds, 81
    Salmon with Pumpkin Sunflower Sauce, 155
    Sweet Potato and Green Bean Salad, 95
    Tropical Granola, 43
Sunny Smoothie, 31
Survivor Bowl, 39
Sweet Potato and Green Bean Salad, 95
sweet potatoes, 22
    Sweet Potato and Green Bean Salad, 95
swordfish
    Spiced Swordfish Skewers, 159

T
Tacos Pico de Gallo, 195
Tapioca Crepe with Tomato Mozzarella, 55
Tapioca Pearl Pudding, 212
Tequila Gravlax, 59
thyme
    Moroccan Rubbed Red Snapper with Apricot and Hazelnut Sauce, 152–153
tilapia
    Fish with Pepita Sauce, 161
tomatillo, 22–23

Chicken Stew with Tomatillos and Cilantro, 137
Fish with Pepita Sauce, 161
tomatoes
    Arroz con Pollo, 112–113
    Baião de Dois (Stir Fry Brazilian Style), 175
    Brazilian Guacamole, 47
    Ceviche with Tiger's Milk, 73
    Chicken Barley Stew, 124–125
    Chicken in a Pot, 123
    Chicken Tamale Pie, 119–121
    Chicken Tortilla Soup, 101–103
    Fish with Eggplant and Tomato Sauce, 165–166
    Hearts of Palm Ceviche, 67
    Huevos Cubanos, 69
    Picadillo de Pollo, 139
    Quinoa with Chicken Sausage and Mushrooms,
        144–145
    Ricotta-Stuffed Zucchini, 198
    Ropa Vieja de Pollo, 115–116
    Sardines with Tomato Olive Salsa, 168
    Sopa Seca, 99
    Tacos Pico de Gallo, 195
    Tapioca Crepe with Tomato Mozzarella, 55
    Tortilla Espanola, 51
    Turkey with Mole Sauce, 129–131
Tomato Sauce
    Kale Gnocchi, 74–75
Tortilla Espanola, 51
tortillas
    Broccoli Fajitas with Cashew, 192
    Chicken Tortilla Soup, 101–103
    Spinach Mushroom Quesadilla, 71
    Tacos Pico de Gallo, 195
Tropical Granola, 43
turkey, 15
    Chicken Tamale Pie, 119–121
    Picadillo de Pollo, 139
    Turkey with Mole Sauce, 129–131
Turkey Sausage with Bell Peppers, 118
Turkey with Mole Sauce, 129–131
turmeric
    Farofa, 183
    Fish Moqueca with Banana, Cashews, and
        Cilantro, 162–163

V

vegetable stock
    Hearty Black Bean Soup, 97
vinegar

balsamic
    Fish with Eggplant and Tomato Sauce,
        165–166
white wine
    Bok Choy Salad with Sunflower Seeds, 81
    Hearts of Palm and Spinach Salad, 85
    Orange Salad with Pumpkin Seeds and
        Crumbled Queso-Blanco, 93
    Wheatberry Waldorf Salad, 89

W

walnuts
    Butternut Mash with Arugula Pesto, 187
Warm Cucumber Chicken Salad, 117
watercress
    Fish with Eggplant and Tomato Sauce, 165–166
Watercress Flan, 76–78
watermelon, 23
Watermelon Carpaccio with Feta Cheese, Olives,
    Cilantro and Arugula, 107
Wheatberry Waldorf Salad, 89
Whole Wheat Fusilli with Chicken and Avocado
    Cashew Pesto, 178–179
wine
    port
        Chicken in a Pot, 123
    white
        Chicken in a Pot, 123
        Chicken Tamale Pie, 119–121
        Chicken with Peas and Potatoes, 127–128
        Fish Veracruz, 167
        Grilled Chicken Drumstick with Orange
            Glaze, 135
        Picadillo de Pollo, 139
        Quinoa Risotto with Peas and Turkey Bacon,
            181
        Roasted Chicken Breast with Guava BBQ
            Sauce, 140–141
        Ropa Vieja de Pollo, 115–116
        Turkey Sausage with Bell Peppers, 118

Y

yogurt
    Mexican Creamed Corn, 197
    Passion Fruit Eton Mess, 215
yucca, 23–24
    Kale Gnocchi, 74–75
    Tapioca Crepe with Tomato Mozzarella, 55
Yucca Latkes, 183